D0184653

JULIUS CAESAR

JULIUS CAESAR

PAT SOUTHERN

TEMPUS

First published 2001

PUBLISHED IN THE UNITED KINGDOM BY:

Tempus Publishing Ltd
The Mill, Brimscombe Port
Stroud, Gloucestershire GL5 2QG

PUBLISHED IN THE UNITED STATES OF AMERICA BY:

Arcadia Publishing Inc.
A division of Tempus Publishing Inc.
2 Cumberland Street
Charleston, SC 29401
1-888-313-2665

Tempus books are available in France, Germany and Belgium
from the following addresses:

Tempus Publishing Group	Tempus Publishing Group	Tempus Publishing Group
21 Avenue de la République	Gustav-Adolf-Straße 3	Place de L'Alma 4/5
37300 Joué-lès-Tours	99084 Erfurt	1200 Brussels
FRANCE	GERMANY	BELGIUM

© Pat Southern, 2001

The right of Pat Southern to be identified as the Author
of this work has been asserted by her in accordance with the
Copyrights, Designs and Patents Act 1988.

All rights reserved. No part of this book may be reprinted or reproduced or utilised
in any form or by any electronic, mechanical or other means, now known or
hereafter invented, including photocopying and recording, or in any information
storage or retrieval system, without the permission in writing from the Publishers.

British Library Cataloguing in Publication Data.
A catalogue record for this book is available from the British Library.

ISBN 0 7524 1443 7

Typesetting and origination by Tempus Publishing.
PRINTED AND BOUND IN GREAT BRITAIN

Contents

List of illustrations

Introduction and acknowledgements

There are many books on Caesar. Some of them concentrate on the political aspects of his career, others on his military genius. His life has been depicted in many forms. There are scholarly books that support every statement with ancient evidence and modern opinion. There are plays, novels and films; Shakespeare's Caesar, George Bernard Shaw's Caesar, Rex Warner's novel, among many others; and Rex Harrison's witty, urbane conquering Caesar. There is the Caesar of the Asterix books: 'It is well known that Caesar had a lot of Gaul'. Perhaps he would have been amused. There are as many Caesars as there are biographies. He has no parallel in any era, because he had no ancient parallel, and ever since his death each era has rewritten him according to the prevailing morals and customs. There is an eternal fascination about him; love him or hate him, indifference is not applicable to Caesar.

The portraits of Caesar from ancient times are not impartial, and mostly present aspects of him as seen by the individual or corporate onlooker, with all the attendant bias for or against. Though he wrote accounts of the Gallic war and the civil war, there is little of himself in them except the self-advertisement that he wished to display. We know what Caesar did; we do not know who he was. Certain features stand out but do not make up the whole person: the sheer staggering driving energy of the man, the ruthlessness and determination to achieve what he wanted, the loyalty that he inspired in some people and the extreme hatred that he inspired in others. He came close to being defeated in battle, but never lost a war. He caused the deaths of many people, but did not proscribe thousands, like Marius and Sulla before him and Antony and Octavian after him. His aim was to improve, augment and streamline the administration of Rome and the provinces. To do that he needed supreme power, and in achieving it he formed the bridge between the Roman Republic and the Roman Empire.

Hence yet another book, to complete the trilogy with *Mark Antony* and *Cleopatra*. This one might never have been written if Peter Kemmis Betty had not suggested it and kept on phoning spasmodically to see if it was progressing. There would not have been a book if Jacqui Taylor and Jan Shearsmith had said no when I asked them to do drawings. Similarly I am grateful to David Brearley for providing photos, and to the Ny

Carlsberg Glyptotek, Copenhagen; the Berlin Antikensammlung, Berlin Museen; the Capitoline Museum, Rome; the Vatican Museum; the Musée Archéologique de Narbonne; and the V & A Photographic library.

1 Apprenticeship

Caesar: a name known to almost everyone, with or without the slightest interest in Roman history. As a title it evokes the Emperors of the Roman world, if not the one man who started it all, and it is perpetuated into the twenty-first century in the designations that instantly proclaim Imperialism on the grand scale. In Latin, the name Caesar was pronounced with a hard C, and the 'ae' rhymed with 'eye'; Kaiser Bill and Tsar Nicholas were the last in a long line of rulers who derived their titles with scarcely altered phonetics from a remarkable man called Gaius Julius Caesar, who was born in 100 BC and assassinated in 44.

Most of the major ancient sources agree on the year in which Caesar was born, but not the exact date, which narrows down to a choice between 12 July (Suetonius, Appian and Plutarch) and 13 July (Dio). The family of the Julii were patricians, but had not so far produced any famous politicians or military commanders. The result of this obscurity is that next to nothing is known of Caesar's ancestors. His father, also Gaius Julius Caesar, died young, without having reached the consulship. Had he lived longer he may have attained this goal; he had been praetor and gone on to the prestigious post of proconsul of Asia, one in which it was possible to amass not a little wealth by various means. Caesar was only 15 years old when his father died, and so his upbringing devolved upon his mother Aurelia whose relatives included consuls, but not very notable or notorious ones. She was of the family of the Aurelii Cottae, perhaps the cousin of Gaius, Lucius, and Marcus Aurelius Cotta, consuls respectively in 75, 74 and 65. The most influential member of Caesar's family while he was a child and adolescent was his uncle Gaius Marius, a self-made man who rose to prominence via the army. He was of middle class or equestrian birth, but entered the Senate and went on to various magistracies with the help of his connections with Scipio Aemilianus and the powerful family of the Metelli. He married Julia, the sister of Gaius Julius Caesar the elder and therefore Caesar's aunt, about ten or twelve years before his famous nephew was born. His influence on Caesar has not been quantified, but his career paved the way for the civil wars from which Caesar emerged the sole victor in the 40s BC.

Marius was a new man, a *novus homo* like Cicero, with no famous forebears or attested aristocratic ancestors. Such men had to rely upon

1   *Head of Gaius Julius Caesar, idealised and perhaps not contemporary, but one of the most famous portraits.* Courtesy Vatican Museums, Vatican City

their own merits and talents to rise in the political world of Rome. Marius began as a soldier and exhibited a marked aptitude for warfare; he fought with Scipio in Spain at the siege of Numantia, and in 109 he was chosen by Quintus Caecilius Metellus Numidicus as his legate in the war against Jugurtha in Africa. In 108 he requested leave of absence from this war to return to Rome for the consular elections for 107; Metellus thought little of his chances and made no secret of his views; he was probably worried that his own reputation as Marius' patron might suffer, but his scepticism was unfounded. Marius was elected; it no doubt cost a lot of money and involved much whispering into peoples' ears, orchestrated by Marius and his circle of friends and clients. He returned to Africa to try to subdue Jugurtha, but the rebel leader used his knowledge of the terrain and his rapid mobility to evade defeat and capture. When he was finally entrapped after two years of fighting it was by treachery, organised by Marius' quaestor, Lucius Cornelius Sulla, and

Jugurtha's own father-in-law Bocchus, who handed him over to the Romans.

Had it not been for external threats to Rome's safety, Marius' career might have peaked during the Jugurthine war, and subsided thereafter, with perhaps a second consulship and some significant political contribution engineered by himself to satisfy his ambition. He could have sought a province where he could embark on new conquests, as Caesar did in the 50s after his consulship. But soon after his return from Africa Marius was called upon to defend Rome from her most terrifying enemies, the Celtic tribes who had been roaming through Italy and Gaul since *c*.113. They invaded Italy in 104 and on several occasions in ensuing years. The consular elections were scarcely contested. Year after year Marius was appointed consul and given powers to deal with the emergencies. There was no real choice in the matter, but prolonged commands such as this had become more common and set the precedent for others in the future.

Marius drew upon his experience of the army to improve its performance. He built on the ideas of Publius Rutilius Rufus, consul in 105, whose task was to rebuild the army and its confidence after the Celtic tribes inflicted a terrible defeat on the Romans near Arausio (modern Orange) in Gaul. Rufus instituted arms drill, something that commanders of regular standing armies would take for granted. One of the problems that Rome faced in any war was her lack of a permanent army of paid professional soldiers. While Rome was a self-contained city state without provinces to defend, the time-honoured system worked tolerably well; when wars threatened it was usual to call the citizen-farmers to arms for the duration of the campaigns and then send them all home when the war was concluded. The accretion of provinces made Rome into a small Empire rather than a city state, and on the other side of the ever widening boundaries there were new peoples and new perceived threats requiring armies in different parts of the Roman world, sometimes simultaneously. The Italian allies provided troops for the army, and Rome employed mercenaries as well, but these were not part of the Roman army proper which consisted of Roman citizens who owned land. This restrictive practice created problems; the small farmers who were conscripted faced ruin because they were absent from their farms for too long, while a potential source of recruits was ignored, namely the urban poor. The property qualification had already been reduced, but now Marius removed it altogether from the recruitment process, supplementing conscription by means of voluntary enlistment, thus widening the recruitment base and solving the manpower shortage after exhausting wars had depleted numbers. It was a sensible measure, and no doubt someone else would have thought of it sooner or later, but before it could be put into operation the state had to find the necessary funds to provide equipment for the landless men; the citizen-farmers had always provided their own. In the transitional stages, there were probably discontented grumblings from the old soldiers who witnessed the new ones coming into the ranks, streetwise but without any knowledge of which end of a plough was which, and without having to dig into their own pockets to kit themselves out.

Marius was not simply interested in numbers. He concerned himself with the soldiers' well-being while they served in the ranks, and also their welfare when they were discharged. The first consideration involved putting his practical knowledge to work in improving military organisation; he reduced the cumbersome baggage trains and made the soldiers carry most of their tools and equipment. While he was in Africa fighting against Jugurtha he had been chasing a very mobile enemy who knew and used the terrain to good effect, and the Cimbri and Teutones who threatened Gaul and Italy were no less nimble. In this kind of warfare there were no main cities to besiege and take, no objective to aim for save that of following and trying to second-guess what the enemy would do next, so he needed self-sufficient troops, fast-moving, ready for action at all times, not reliant upon supply and baggage trains. The soldiers applied their own description to these new developments, calling themselves Marius' mules. The second concept — settlement of veterans when campaigns were concluded — was a perennial problem. When the citizen farmer-soldiers came home from the wars they had lands to which they could return. Despite the fact that the aforementioned lands could well have been ruined by the time their owners came back, the state could wash its hands of any responsibility for them, because technically the discharged soldiers had some means of making a living. Volunteer soldiers without property returned to nothing, neither farm nor future, so their only hope of recompense and settlement lay with their commander, just as their commander relied upon their efforts to bring him success. This mutual dependence of commander and soldiers by-passed both Rome herself and the Senate, laying the foundations for the build up and expansion of personal power. The Senate's abhorrence of such private empire-building did not lead directly to avoidance tactics, such as the development of a corporate programme of veteran settlement and the initiation of regular pension schemes for retired soldiers. That only came about late in the reign of Caesar's heir and successor, Augustus, who in AD 6 established the *aerarium militari*, literally the military treasury, with a hefty injection of his own cash to set it up, and a 5% inheritance tax to keep it going. The years between the establishment of Marius' volunteer army and Augustus' military treasury were fraught with the recurring problems of veteran settlement and the associated land questions.

It was the problem of veteran settlement that brought Marius down. In 100 he was elected consul again, though his military services were no longer necessary; by 102 he had eradicated the danger from the tribes of Cimbri and Teutones, in two battles at Aix-en-Provence and in the following year at Vercellae near Milan. His latest consulship was probably partly honorific and partly habit on the part of the voters; Marius intended to use it to oversee the grant of lands to his soldiers. His African veterans from the Jugurthine war had been given lands in 103 through the agency of the tribune Lucius Appuleius Saturninus, so in 100 Marius hoped to be able to repeat the process. Saturninus was tribune again in that year, and his friend Caius Servilius Glaucia was praetor. It seemed as though Marius would be successful, even though his erstwhile patron Metellus opposed the bill and was driven into exile. Saturninus and Glaucia were no doubt pleased at this result, since Metellus had tried to oust them from the Senate because of their inflammatory behaviour throughout the years 103 to 101. Perhaps this history of disruption and violence should have been a warning to Marius, or perhaps he thought himself more than a match for his colleagues, who could be used while they were necessary and then discarded. But they showed alarming ambitions, beyond the limited projects that Marius had in mind. Saturninus broadened his bill to include plans to create colonies and put into effect land settlements for other troops from other theatres of war besides the recent campaigns against the Celtic tribes. So far, this was not at all a bad idea, but in 99, to use a modern colloquialism, it all went pear-shaped. Ambition for political power now unveiled itself, far beyond the original modest plans for reform and for veteran settlement. Saturninus was tribune once more; Glaucia aimed at the consulship. Marius blocked him. Emotions ran amok, riots ensued, the Senate proclaimed a state of emergency and passed the *senatus consultum ultimum* or last decree, and so Marius found himself in the position of having to suppress the men who were so recently his allies. They surrendered to him and were locked into the Senate House; perhaps Marius hoped to protect them. If so, he failed; the mob broke in through the roof and Saturninus and Glaucia were killed. Fortunately for Marius and his soldiers, the land settlements were not impeded, but after having reached the pinnacle of military and political fame, Marius plunged from zenith to nadir overnight. This was the era and the family into which Caesar was born.

It was a turbulent period of foreign wars, internal strife, escalating violence and rapid shifts of power and influence. Within the state recurring problems were continually tackled by various individuals who introduced bills designed to alleviate one or sometimes all the ills that beset sections of the community. These included the land question; the food supply; the extension of citizenship to the Italian allies who had helped Rome in her wars; the diminished power of the Senate; the growing influence of the equestrian class; these were all potential flash points during Caesar's early boyhood. Over three decades before he was born, Tiberius Sempronius Gracchus and his younger brother Gaius had tried to solve the land question and a number of related issues, rationalising land ownership and redistributing plots of surplus land to the urban poor. Tiberius was tribune in 133 and drew up a bill encompassing most of the land problems. He tried to circumvent senatorial opposition to his bill by taking it directly to the popular assembly. This in itself was not such an unprecedented or objectionable procedure, but what followed took Tiberius Gracchus somewhat beyond his brief. Another tribune, Marcus Octavius, vetoed his proposals, so Tiberius removed him from office. This enormity was hardly opposed at the time, but when Tiberius announced his intention to seek election to the tribunate for the following year, opposition increased and hardened; one never knew where Tiberius' ambition would take him next, and his reputation for getting all his own way by force warned people off. He was killed in 132. His brother Gaius emerged a decade later with wider-ranging ideas for distribution of land, foundation of colonies, and the food supply of the urban poor in Rome. He also advocated the grant of citizenship to the Latin colonies and the extension of Latin rights, regarded as a halfway stage to full Roman citizenship, to the Italians. The grant of Roman citizenship did not mean that the recipients had to give up their own citizenship of whichever city they lived in and go to live in Rome; Roman citizenship was valued because of its legal privileges and its immunity from certain punishments. It included the right to exercise the vote, though for that it was necessary to travel to Rome, which was not always possible, especially at harvest time or in winter. The road to enfranchisement for the Italian allies was long and frustrating. Three years before Gaius Gracchus introduced his bill, Marcus Fulvius Flaccus had failed in the same purpose, so it was certain that there would be opposition. Like Tiberius before him, Gaius tried to have his laws passed by force, meeting his adversaries with an army. He too was killed, along with many of his supporters, in 121. Politics in Rome had never been the most peaceful of scenarios, but now violence and murder had become part of political life.

When Caesar was about eight or nine years old, another politician made an attempt to solve these perennial problems. Marcus Livius Drusus was tribune in 91, and his proposals were designed to solve nearly all the interrelated problems that the Gracchi and others had failed to solve. He added another dimension in that his plans included the elevation of 300 equites to the Senate, which on the face of it seems to suggest that he was interested in establishing social mobility and rewarding worthy members of the middle classes, but it was a means of reducing the influence of the equites, whose often venal business interests formed an important element in foreign policy. It was the equites who derived, or more correctly extorted, the most profit out of the provincials; by turning the most influential of the equites into senators, the influence of the class as a whole would be diluted, and the influence of the 300 new senators would not be sufficient to compensate for the dilution at a higher level. At the same time, the promotion of equites to senatorial status would curtail their particular business activities and force them to make new alliances, since senators were not allowed to engage in anything so sordid as work, trade, or any other business, and did so only through their equestrian agents. But senators did not always command the unswerving loyalty of their equestrian agents, unless they played the game and allowed them to profit from Rome's conquests. Provincials who suffered as a result of equestrian or senatorial extortion could not recoup their losses by appealing to the law, since the equestrians had been placed in charge of the jury courts from the time of the Gracchi, and as a class they had failed to exercise impartiality in cases that might jeopardise their freedom to make even more profit from provincial conquests.

Contained in Drusus' bill there was a clause concerning citizenship for the Italian allies. For over thirty years the question had been raised and dropped, and the Italians were no closer to achieving their goal; this time, although the laws had been passed, the consul Lucius Marcius Philippus had them annulled, and then Drusus was killed. The Italian cities lost patience with Roman vacillation. Despairing of ever sharing in the Roman commonwealth as citizens, they went to war.

The battles of the Social War, as it was termed, lasted from 90 to 89, with sundry skirmishing and political manoeuvring rumbling on until 87. The Social War had nothing to do with social classes in the modern sense; it derived its title from the Latin for allies (*socii*). The exasperated Italians began the proceedings with the massacre of all the Romans in Asculum, and although there was a last minute attempt at negotiation the situation escalated into full-scale war. The two main peoples that broke with Rome were Marsi and the Samnites, but eventually the fighting spread to all parts of the peninsula, though some of the allies remained faithful to Rome and were rewarded later. The Romans were at a disadvantage for perhaps the first time, in that the enemy knew exactly how the Roman army fought, and was more familiar with the terrain than their adversaries. The war was brought to an end by the timely grant of citizenship, but this did not come about because Rome had suddenly adopted an attitude of benevolence. A war was looming in the east, so in order to provide an army to attend to this problem, the current war in

Italy must be concluded as soon as possible. In 89 the *lex Plautia Papiria* was passed granting Roman citizenship to all Italians south of the river Po, and Pompeius Strabo, the father of Pompey who styled himself the Great, and who became Caesar's ally then his enemy, passed another law granting Latin rights, or what amounted to half citizenship, to the tribes who lived immediately north of the Po, the Transpadane Gauls. This provided an area ripe for an enterprising politician who required support outside Rome, and Caesar tried to gain full citizen rights for the Transpadanes as soon as he had the opportunity, about a decade later. Suetonius states that he encouraged them to agitate for full citizenship, implying that Caesar would not have hesitated to stir up rebellion, but he was discouraged by the presence of troops. This is nonsensical; Caesar wanted clients who were bound to him by gratitude, and to encourage open rebellion was not the way to go about it.

The Social War receded in importance as the eastern provinces came under threat from Mithridates VI Eupator, king of Pontus. Rome had already had some dealings with him and his aggressive expansionist policies. While most of Italy was aflame and Rome was very preoccupied, Mithridates invaded the province of Asia, having overrun Bithynia and Cappadocia. The Greek cities of the east welcomed him, because the Romans were rapacious masters who had reached new heights in exploiting the wealth of the east, and there was no redress to be gained by appealing to Roman lawyers and the courts. The Romans and Italians who had set up businesses in the east were massacred to a man. Even if the numbers of dead were exaggerated at Rome it was clear that this was not an invasion that could be called off by negotiation. The command was given to one of the generals who had distinguished himself in the Social War, the man who had intrigued with Bocchus to capture Jugurtha, consul for 88, Lucius Cornelius Sulla. At this point Marius re-entered politics, because he wanted the command for himself. He allied himself with Publius Sulpicius Rufus who was tribune in 88. It was a mutually supportive coalition. Sulpicius Rufus had an agenda of his own; he planned to continue the work of his friend Livius Drusus on behalf of the newly enfranchised Italians. His proposal ran counter to senatorial policy in that he advocated the distribution of the new citizens equally among all the 35 voting tribes, so that their influence in politics would not be diluted and meaningless. He successfully transferred the command against Mithridates to Marius, and passed his laws, not without the violence that was now customary in these emotive times. None of his laws enjoyed a prolonged shelf-life, because Sulla gathered the army that he was assembling for the eastern war and marched on Rome at the head of it. Marius fled to Africa, Sulpicius was killed, and the laws were annulled. The enormity of marching on Rome was such that most of Sulla's officers, except his kinsman Lucius Licinius Lucullus, refused to be involved. Once in Rome, Sulla passed laws quickly and easily, quickly because he was anxious to start the eastern campaign without delay, and easily because the presence of his troops, patently more loyal to him than they were to the abstract idea of Rome, tended to silence any opposition. Caesar was just entering his teens; perhaps he noted the efficacy of armed law-making. As a young boy he would not attract too much attention from Sulla at this time, but he was indelibly dyed with the colours of Marius and could hardly pretend to be otherwise inclined.

Sulla was either unable or unwilling to prevent the election of his enemy Lucius Cornelius Cinna as one of the consuls for 87. Since the other consul was Gnaeus Octavius, who opposed Cinna and his policies, perhaps Sulla thought that there would be nothing to fear, and that Octavius would keep his rival in check. He left Rome for the east after having extracted a promise from Cinna not to undo his recent laws. He could not afford to stay any longer, because the edifice he had built was too fragile to be sustained unless he was prepared to continue as he had begun. Escaping prosecution, he went off to war; if he was defeated then he would lose nothing, but if he was victorious he could return as conquering hero and saviour. Only time would tell. No sooner had he left than trouble broke out in Rome. Octavius deposed Cinna, and drove him out of Rome, but Cinna had like-minded friends, and access to soldiers, so he emulated Sulla and attacked Rome. Marius joined him, and so did Quintus Sertorius and Gnaeus Papirius Carbo, who were to play starring roles in the later fighting. The consul Octavius relied on the armies of Pompeius Strabo and Quintus Caecilius Metellus Pius, but Strabo died, somehow. Judging by the fact that his body was dragged ignominiously through the streets by an angry mob, it is questionable whether his death was altogether natural. Dead from an epidemic, say some sources; struck by lightning, say others, but that would have conferred a kind of divinity among the superstitious. Without Strabo and his army, Metellus Pius was ineffective. Towards the end of 87, with Marius in his entourage, Cinna took Rome. A period of total carnage followed as Marius exacted revenge on all and sundry. In the lawlessness of the times, no doubt old scores were settled by many people under the general heading of Marius' pogrom. In 86, having been made consul with Cinna, Marius died. It was an inglorious end to an illustrious career.

Caesar was drawn into this circle by Cinna. He was made a priest of Jupiter, *flamen Dialis*, after the office-holder Lucius Cornelius Merula died. Caesar probably took up this post in 84 when he turned 16 and became legally an adult; he would undergo the ceremony that marked the transition from boyhood to manhood, where he exchanged the dress of a minor, the *toga praetexta*, for the dress of a man, the *toga virilis*. The *flamen Dialis* could not marry any other than a patrician woman, so the betrothal to the daughter of an equestrian was broken off, and Caesar married Cinna's daughter Cornelia, who gave birth in 76 to his only legitimate child, Julia. Cornelia remained his wife until 69 when she died.

By the end of 85, Caesar had lost his father and was consequently the man of the household, under the tutelage of his mother Aurelia. As *flamen Dialis* he was in a privileged and honourable position, but destined for a restricted life, subject to antiquated laws and customs. He was forbidden to ride a horse or to witness any military activity. His career might never have progressed at all if he had remained in office, but perhaps he had no intention of remaining in it, and acquiesced only until something better presented itself. The priesthood could have been a stepping stone to a patrician political career, but for the unfortunate enmity between the party of Cinna and that of Sulla. In the absence of the latter, Cinna held on to the consulship for a second and third term in 85 and 84, with Papirius Carbo as his colleague; he did so by force, not willing to risk his policies to chance and the uncertainties of re-election. Three consecutive years as consul gave him the means to force through his legislation and to control and guide the state in the direction he thought it should go. This was a phenomenon that had occurred in the past when the Gracchi sought continuity as tribunes in order to put into operation their land distribution bills and other legislation; Saturninus repeated the attempt and his colleague Glaucia aimed for the consulship, not just to gratify personal ambition but to give themselves the power and above all the time to implement their policies and laws. The system of annual elections of consuls and other magistrates was designed to prevent anyone from gaining too much personal power, but it had its drawbacks, already demonstrated in the past whenever continuity was necessary, as for instance when Marius was elected consul again and again, even in his absence, in order to conduct the prolonged wars against the Celtic tribes in the north.

Caesar's life during these early years is not well documented, no doubt because his talents had not yet revealed themselves and no one had seen in him anything out of the ordinary. He presumably gave some thought to what would happen when Sulla returned from the east, especially since he was in entirely the wrong camp and could hardly pretend to be neutral, being allied to the late Marius and to Cinna as his son-in-law. It may have helped that Cinna was killed in a mutiny late in 84, so that by the time Sulla reached Rome, Caesar could stand almost alone. He did not ally himself closely with Cinna's deputy Carbo, who took over the leadership of Cinna's party. Nor did Caesar embroil himself with his kinsman Marius the younger when he was elected consul in 82 with Carbo as colleague; in fact the family disapproved of the younger Marius' plans.

Sulla rounded off his successful war against Mithridates and landed in Italy in 84. He fought his way towards Rome, joined by Marius' enemy Quintus Caecilius Metellus Pius, Marcus Licinius Crassus, and a young man of 23 who had raised three legions from his father's veterans and tenants from his estates in Picenum; this was Gnaeus Pompeius, better known in English as Pompey, young, handsome, bursting with confidence, brutally efficient, nauseatingly successful and ruthlessly ambitious. Within two or three years he was calling himself Magnus, the Great. From now onwards he would form a large element in Caesar's life, though it would be two decades before they came into close association. In 83 Pompey and his army won victories for Sulla; he went on to chase Papirius Carbo to Sicily where he eliminated him, bloodily, earning the name *adulescentulus carnifex* (young butcher). Then he went on to Africa to fight against Domitius Ahenobarbus. No anti-Sullans were to survive, except Sertorius in Spain. Pompey came home in 81 and demanded a triumph, for which he was too young, had not gone through the proper career structure, and was hopelessly unqualified except for the incontrovertible facts that he had won lots of battles and knew how to sell himself. Sulla had by this time established himself in Rome and placed himself firmly at the head of the government; he was trying to bring the city and the provinces back to orthodox procedures. He refused Pompey's triumph, at which the young man had a tantrum and burst out with the retort that more people worshipped the rising sun than the setting sun, thus making it clear what he thought of their relative positions. Instead of executing him there and then, Sulla let him have his triumph. The only disappointment after that was the unforeseen problem that the elephants that Pompey wanted to draw his chariot would not fit through the arches on the way to the Forum and the Sacred Way, so he had to make do with horses like ordinary mortals.

Caesar was bound to come to the attention of Sulla sooner or later. The sole sacrifice that Sulla demanded of him was that he should divorce his wife Cornelia. That would mean that with the elder Marius and Cinna both dead, and the fact that Caesar had not allied himself to Carbo, there would be little connection with the pre-Sullan regime. Perhaps it would be possible to win the young man over. But it was not. Caesar refused to divorce Cornelia and went into hiding. He may have been in love with Cornelia, overriding any sense of pragmatism, but most probably he wished to make a demonstration of independence. He made his point, but his only rewards were malaria, contracted in the marshy country where he chose to hide, followed by capture. Fortunately his

2 *Head of Gnaeus Pompeius Magnus, who rose to fame as a young man by raising*
an army on behalf of Sulla. Caesar allied with him as he entered office as consul,
and forced through legislation to ratify the arrangements that Pompey had made for
the eastern provinces and allied states, and to provide the veteran soldiers with land.
The two men were more closely allied when Pompey married Caesar's daughter
Julia, who died in 54. Courtesy Ny Carlsberg Glyptotek, Copenhagen

mother's relatives, the Aurelii Cottae, were followers of Sulla and spoke
up for him. Cornelia lost her dowry, but the couple were not harmed.
Allegedly, Sulla remarked that the youth should be watched because he
had many Mariuses in him. If it was true that Sulla discerned something
of merit in the 19-year-old Caesar, it is all the more surprising that he
should have spared him, but Caesar at 19 with scarcely any following, no
vast fortune, and no political influence was not to be feared. His father
had reached only the praetorship, and cannot have had much
opportunity to gather a large *clientelae* that his young son could inherit. At
15 years old when his father died Caesar could not be of political or social
assistance to any followers that his father may have cultivated, so all but
the most loyal would have allied themselves with another politician to

further their own careers. Though he may have owned estates and farms, it does not seem that Caesar could call upon thousands of adherents, as could Pompey from among his father's veterans and tenants. Nor could he draw on reserves of ready cash such as Crassus had set about amassing for himself. As yet he could be no threat to Sulla. Despite the retrospective legend that Caesar was marked out for an illustrious career almost from the cradle, at 19 he was more isolated than most, a situation that perhaps goes some way to explain his individuality and independence in later life. From Suetonius' account he emerges as something of a poseur, distinctive in dress, not just fashion-conscious but a decadent trend setter, with a loose belt round his tunic and fringes dangling from hems and sleeves, not at all conservative in appearance or attitude. He did not associate inextricably either with rebels on the one hand or with wealthy patrons on the other, nor did he enter into any situations from which he could not detach himself with reasonably clean hands. He trusted only himself, perhaps a few friends, and his immediate family. This isolation only serves to illustrate how far he had to go to rise to any heights at all.

In 81 he removed himself from close proximity to Sulla, having obtained an appointment on the staff of Marcus Minucius Thermus, propraetor of Asia. The war against Mithridates was not completely won, mostly because Mithridates had not been killed and had not renounced his ambitions in the east. It follows that any officers and governors in that region would be Sullan partisans who would continue the work that he had started. Thermus was such a man, so it would seem that Caesar obtained his post with Sulla's blessing. Young Romans most commonly began their careers in this way, combining military and civilian posts in a way that modern specialists would find disconcerting. Most of these offices did not demand any experience; they bestowed it. Caesar remained in the east until Sulla's death. His first major task was a diplomatic one, when he was sent to the court of king Nicomedes IV of Bithynia. It was important to keep the kings of the surrounding territories well disposed to Rome, in case they should find in Mithridates a more promising ally. It was a reciprocal agreement, so when the Romans required ships to augment their fleet in the war against Mytilene, they looked to Nicomedes to provide them. Caesar was sent to take possession of them. This meeting with Nicomedes was to dog Caesar's footsteps all his life, since it was rumoured that he had a homosexual relationship with the king. It was not an unusual accusation in Roman politics, but most young men were accused of mundane relationships with other Roman politicians; Caesar's alleged relationship was more exotic, with a king, no less. The only difference in political life for the past 2000 years is the perception of the scandal; Caesar's reputation was not harmed by the stories, and he did not bother too strenuously to deny them until his triumph later in his career, when he seems to have given vent to considerable anger about it.

Once he had brought the ships to join the Roman efforts against Mytilene, the main city of the Greek island of Lesbos, Caesar tasted military action for the first time, earning a decoration for bravery in the process when the city was taken. This was the *corona civica* awarded to those who had saved the lives of Roman citizens in battle. Privileges as well as honours came with the award. The recipient was released from civic obligations, and when he entered the auditorium at the games, everyone including senators stood in his honour.

While Caesar was absent in the east, Sulla strengthened his regime in Rome. He became Dictator, an office that was normally held for six months but in Sulla's case was extended indefinitely until the emergency was over. Proscriptions followed his entry into Rome, worse than anything Marius and Cinna had perpetrated. No one was safe because people used the opportunity to rid themselves of their personal rivals by adding the names of their enemies to the lists. No one bothered to check on the authenticity of the lists. Sulla had already passed some laws before he left Rome for the Mithridatic war, but in the interim Cinna had been at work, so it was probable that Sulla had to start all over again. He had had more opportunity than most men to assess the problems that beset the state, not least because he had caused some of them himself by flouting long-established customs and laws. Now he set about finding the remedies. He tried to shore up the government so that no one else could emulate him. One of the first measures was to muzzle the tribunate, though it is not clear precisely how he did so. It may be that he simply passed a law requiring tribunes to bring their bills before the Senate instead of taking them to the people's assembly, but his most restrictive measure was to truncate the career of anyone who wished to become a tribune by forbidding access to any other office. Ambitious men who hoped to use the tribunate as a springboard for a career would find that avenue blocked. Sulla followed Livius Drusus' plan to elevate 300 equites to the Senate, doubling the traditional number of senators, and he returned the jury courts to the Senate. As Rome increased her Empire, more personnel were required to govern the provinces and take on the functions of the magistrates in Rome itself. The turnover of provincial commands had been less rapid than desirable, involving long-standing governorships that led to a build up of personal influence in one province. The enlarged Senate would provide more candidates to fill all the necessary posts; henceforth there were to be eight praetors and 20 quaestors, and upon becoming quaestor young men automatically entered the Senate, a move which was to benefit Caesar when the time came. But somewhat retrograde measures constituted a potential hindrance to him. Sulla decreed that there should be specified intervals between magistracies, with the result that no one could reach the consulship until his early forties. This was designed to combat the rapid rise of politicians and generals who swept through the career structure by progressing from office to office with scarcely an interval. In the case of Pompey it was ineffectual, but in Caesar's case circumstances rather than laws ensured that he progressed slowly towards the consulship, reaching it only two years short of the specified age.

Though Sulla put into practice some of the ideas of Livius Drusus, and settled his own veterans in Campania, he did not institute any state system for regular settlement of veterans or pension schemes when soldiers from various wars were discharged. Thus he did not provide a standing army, paid and protected by the state, and more importantly he did not remove the danger posed by armies whose loyalties were firmly directed towards a commander rather than to Rome. He also left enclaves of discontented men who had been displaced in order to accommodate his own soldiers on the land. These men would follow anyone who promised them redress and new lands for themselves. A reasonable policy of veteran settlement would have solved the two problems at once, alleviating distress of the soldiers without displacing anyone. Ultimately what Sulla had done was to emphasise rather than quell the client system, diluting the stern Roman sense of duty to the Senate and People of Rome, and substituting for it a partisan scramble for power among the leading men whose reliance upon their clients and connections was now even more important than it had ever been before.

When his work was done, and he felt that in accordance with a prophecy he was approaching death, Sulla resigned in 79. Caesar was said to have considered this action ludicrous, though this is perhaps not a contemporary opinion, but one formed later when he had tasted power for himself. Sulla died in 78. In that year Caesar had just obtained a post under the command of Publius Servilius Isauricus in Cilicia, in operations against the ubiquitous pirates who congregated there. He may have made the acquaintance of Titus Labienus, serving under the same command. Labienus was a native of Picenum, Pompey's territory, but he cooperated with Caesar in political manoeuvres in 64, and followed him to Gaul. After only a short time as an officer under Servilius, Caesar returned to Rome, in haste according to Suetonius, because when the news of Sulla's death reached him, and also news of the rebellious activities of the consul of 78, Marcus Aemilius Lepidus, who was intent on neutralising the Sullan regime, he thought he might be able to profit from the situation. Either Suetonius is completely mistaken, or Caesar assessed Lepidus' chances of success and found them wanting. He kept a low profile and did not play any part in the ill-advised rebellion. Lepidus agitated for reform of Sulla's laws as soon as the latter was dead, but met with opposition from his colleague Quintus Lutatius Catulus. Instead of acting resolutely and quickly, Lepidus vacillated, contacting anti-Sullan elements such as Sertorius who had carved out a personal empire in Spain, and then the displaced farmers and other parties in Italy who had a grudge against Sulla. When fighting finally broke out, Catulus defeated Lepidus, and Pompey emerged as a conquering hero once again. He was given a military command to assist Catulus, but then kept his army together just in case he should be needed to speed to the assistance of Metellus Pius against Sertorius in Spain. The Senate granted his wish and so he marched off to Spain, where he stayed until 71.

Caesar may have sympathised with Lepidus' ideas, but he did nothing to compromise himself, perhaps because he was shrewd enough to see that it was too soon to overturn most of Sulla's work, and that if it were to be done at all it required proper preparation and the assembly of a much larger power base. At any rate, aloofness and circumspection served him well all through his career, and he was not about to sacrifice himself unless it was for a much more secure and certain reason. For the time being he followed a more orthodox path. In 77, on behalf of the people of Macedonia, he brought a prosecution against Gnaeus Cornelius Dolabella for extortion. Many young Romans established their political reputation via the law courts; it was one way of advertising talent and perhaps encouraging the growth of a personal following. Dolabella was one of Sulla's generals who had been with him on the campaign against Mithridates, and had used the opportunity as governor of Macedonia to line his own pockets on a magnificent scale. The fact that a Sullan partisan could be prosecuted with impunity one year after the death of the Dictator says something for Caesar's attitude and for the political climate at Rome, but despite eloquent speeches Caesar did not win his case. His kinsman Gaius Aurelius Cotta and the famous orator Quintus Hortensius defended Dolabella, who had many important friends, or at least enough to secure his acquittal.

Nonetheless, Caesar's reputation was not ruined by losing the case, and in 76 he was asked by other Greeks cities to prosecute Gaius Antonius for extortion. Antonius was plainly guilty and did not have the same influential friends as Dolabella, so he had to resort to an appeal to the tribunes in order to wriggle out of condemnation. In effect Caesar had won his case but did not have the satisfaction of seeing it through to a conviction. Some years later, Caesar supported Gaius Antonius in his bid for the consulship of 63; it was not entirely because Caesar believed Antonius to be the best candidate, but it was a case of supporting the best of a bad lot and blocking the other candidates, Lucius Sergius Catilina and Marcus Tullius Cicero. Staunch unwavering consistency was not a feature of Roman political alliances, which were not based on true friendship; instead pragmatism, expediency and usefulness ruled the day.

Military activity, civil government, and experience of the law courts were all part of a young Roman's upbringing, but there was another element which so far Caesar lacked. This was to go to the equivalent of a university. Some youths went to Athens to round off their education; Caesar went to Rhodes in 75. This is the context of one of the more fabulous episodes in Caesar's life, when he was captured by pirates who based themselves in the many harbours and inlets of Cilicia, and made sea travel risky if not fatal. Caesar was never in doubt as to his own merit and told the pirates that he was worth much more than the ransom they had demanded. Of course it was a sensible move to protest his great value, but it would not have worked if he had been unable to persuade the coastal cities of Asia to put together the required sums. He protested that the cities had a duty to keep the seaways clear and if they had attended to that duty he would never have been in the unenviable position of being held at the mercy of a pack of brigands. It took over a month to raise the cash and Caesar remained with his captors, nonchalantly whittling away his time, reading, sleeping, demanding and probably getting peace and quiet while he did so, and threatening jocularly to execute the pirates when he was finally ransomed. The central character throughout the story, which has lost nothing in the retelling, is Caesar himself, but he would not be alone. He would have slaves to attend to him day and night, and presumably companions to do his bidding and to canvass the Asian cities to ransom him. There were perhaps not many as yet in his circle, but the circumstances permit of the conclusion that he could command the allegiance if not the affection of a variety of agents who could plead convincingly on his behalf and who could be trusted not to leave him in the lurch while they looked for a better alliance.

Once he was released he kept his promise to the pirates. Having extracted money from the coastal communities, he now demanded ships, and assembling them into a small navy he attacked and captured the pirates. He took them to Pergamum and then sought out the governor of Asia Minor, Marcus Juncus, who was in Bithynia, which had been bequeathed to Rome by the term of the late king Nicomedes' will. Marcus Juncus was busy and not much interested in the young man's wishes, so he suggested that the captives should be sold as slaves. Caesar wanted revenge, and most of all he probably wanted to keep his word to the letter in order to preserve his credibility; he had promised to execute the pirates and nothing less would satisfy him. So he returned to Pergamum and crucified them all. Quite how he arranged it is not elucidated. He had no official capacity and therefore no real authority. He was barely 26 years old and had no claim to greatness save the signal honour of the *corona civica* that he had won some years earlier, and that would impress only Roman citizens, not the inhabitants of Rome's eastern provinces. Perhaps he was assisted by the population, who only needed the slightest hint to eliminate pirates who made trading ventures and ordinary travel a dangerous business. Having achieved his ends, Caesar went on to Rhodes.

He had been there for only a short time when Mithridates invaded the Roman province of Asia once again. The king of Pontus was disturbed because Bithynia was to be ruled by Romans instead of a potential ally, or as he would have preferred, one of his own vassals. Caesar left Rhodes, arrived at the scene of action, organised a local army and pushed the invaders back. Superlatives enter the account of his life at this point, and the heroics will have been successively embellished in retrospect as his fame and then his legend grew in stature. Audacity and charisma are inadequate and overworked descriptions that do not touch upon Caesar's organisational skills, combined with belief in himself, that enabled him to persuade local populations to provide ships for use against pirates, and then troops for use against one of the most aggressive and successful kings of the east. There is some slight evidence that he may have been attached to the staff of Marcus Antonius (the father of Mark Antony), on whom the Senate had conferred a special command against the pirates in 74. It may be that Caesar contacted him as he set out from Rhodes, or that his actions were recognised after the event and he was slotted into Antonius' command with appropriate rank. It was not a prolonged appointment, since in 73 Caesar returned to Rome to take up a priesthood left vacant after the death of his relative Gaius Aurelius Cotta.

The college of 15 *pontifices* was a co-opted body; one had to be asked to join what was an exclusive elite of nobles of all ages, and often when a member died his replacement was chosen from among his relatives. For Caesar it was an honour; he was not yet a senator and though it was not unknown for young priests to be co-opted before they entered the Senate, his selection as Cotta's replacement suggests that he had influential connections and had not offended too many powerful men. Though it would be another fourteen years before he entered upon his first consulship, it could be said that in 73 he had arrived on the political and social scene.

2 The path to the consulship

Caesar's co-option to the priesthood in 73 was a personal achievement, but publicly it was overshadowed by the events of that same year. The revolt of Spartacus and the gladiators from Capua tied up Roman armies in Italy for two years, and brought Marcus Licinius Crassus to spurious fame. Caesar was military tribune in 72, and may have seen service with Crassus in this war, but for this there is no firm evidence at all, and the formal association of Caesar and Crassus seems to belong to a later date. While Pompey fought at the side of Metellus Pius against the rebel Sertorius in Spain, struggling with the lack of supplies and the difficulties of the terrain, Crassus concentrated on building up his fortune and lending money, binding ambitious but impecunious aspiring politicians to himself. Money was absolutely essential in Roman politics; Crassus knew better than anyone that it reached parts that armed persuasion could not reach, and if it failed to reach those parts then it could also buy armed persuasion to underline the point in question. He used to say that no man could count himself rich unless he could equip and pay an army. But he had not enjoyed such a resounding military reputation as Pompey, and the command that he received and discharged against Spartacus was not an honourable one. An army of gladiators and slaves was not considered a worthy enemy, and it was something of an unpleasant surprise to the Romans that they were unable to wipe the rebels off the face of the earth in one easy campaign. Spartacus, a Thracian, may possibly have been an auxiliary soldier before he became a gladiator, so he probably knew how the Romans fought and used his knowledge well, but his success in welding together all his followers surely depended upon his character and abilities as a leader. For Crassus, this war was not glorious, and it was certainly not profitable, and further humiliation arose from the suggestion that Lucullus should be recalled from the Danube to deal with the revolt. Even when his campaign was almost concluded, the remains of Spartacus' army fled north and were rounded up and defeated by Pompey on his way home through northern Italy from Spain in 71. Pompey made a great deal of noisy mileage out of his victory, as though no one else had fought against the slave army.

Despite their personal differences Pompey and Crassus cooperated in 71 in an election campaign to secure the consulships for 70. For electioneering read bribery and persuasion, if not corruption and coercion. Crassus had been praetor in 72 and was properly eligible for the consulship, but Pompey was under age, and his only qualification was that of a successful general. After a brief and seemingly innocent display of strength while he camped near the city with his soldiers, Pompey disbanded his army as soon as the Senate abandoned Sulla's rules regarding the strict progression through the normal public offices and the age limit that applied to the consulship. Pompey had always been the exception to Sulla's rules. He became a mere private citizen, but his influence was assured, and no one will have been in any doubt that if he called upon his soldiers to support him they would be ready to serve him at a moment's notice. This consideration may have played a part in the smooth organisation of the eventual land settlements for the veterans of the Spanish war, both those of Metellus Pius' command and Pompey's. No ugly scenes and demagogic speeches were necessary this time to put into effect the settlement programme, so Pompey did not embark on his election campaign with a purely military agenda, dubious motives or sullied hands. He did, however, have one slight problem, one that probably did not cause him any loss of sleep, but since his career so far had been totally anomalous, and he had not held any of the normal offices usually held by senators on the way to the consulship, he had not been party to the workings of the Senate. Consequently he had no idea about senatorial procedures or protocol. To remedy this little defect, and no doubt to maintain credibility, he asked his friend Varro to write it all down for him in an instruction manual. Perhaps he sat up late at night, revising by lamplight before he appeared in the Senate next day. At this stage in his career, the young Pompey was in touch with reality. He knew where his deficiencies lay, he was willing to remedy them, and he was courageous enough to enter on his consulship, aware, but blithely unconcerned, that he did not know everything.

During their joint consulship, Pompey and Crassus dismantled parts of the Sullan legislation, notably restoring the tribunate. There was little enough to do to eradicate the work of Sulla, since previous politicians had already started the process as soon as Sulla was dead. There was one area besides the tribunate that had not been fully remedied; this was the composition of the jury courts. The Gracchi had placed them under the control of the equites, who had a sorry track record, but when the courts were handed back to the Senate, the members of that august body had proved no less partial or corrupt. At the beginning of 70, the notorious Verres returned from his post as governor of Sicily, where he had outshone all previous governors in rapacity and personal greed. Marcus Tullius Cicero eagerly took up the case for the prosecution, even going so far as to visit the scene of the crimes and collect evidence. He wrote five stirring speeches, but after he had delivered the first one, the defence conducted by Quintus Hortensius, with whom he was to lock horns many times, had already crumbled. Thoroughly miffed because he was denied the chance to show off his oratorical talents in a long trial, Cicero published the speeches. He would probably have been amused to find that like Caesar's Commentaries on his wars, his Verrine orations have rarely been out of print for 2000 years, and are now used as optional instruments of torture in Latin lessons in schools and colleges. The major point raised by the trial of Verres was that the deplorable level of exploitation of provincials could not continue unchecked. It never disappeared entirely, and it was highly unlikely that it ever would, but at least the Romans attempted to set up jury courts that would be a little less biased towards the profit seekers.

Caesar's kinsman Lucius Aurelius Cotta put through a bill to reform the composition of the courts, which would henceforth be divided between three elements of society, senators, *equites Romani*, and *tribuni aerarii*. Although the names of the three groups have been preserved, there is no consensus among modern historians as to who the last two groups of jurors were. It may mean that only equites who were entitled to receive the public horse (an antiquated means of equipping the cavalry at public expense) were to be enrolled as jurors, but none of this is certain. The *tribuni aerarii* were originally officials of the treasury (*aerarium*), but this post seems to have gone out of use before 70, and the title may have been revived specifically for the jury courts. Whatever the distinction was, the law was passed in an attempt to make the courts less uniformly biased. Since the new *lex Aurelia* was the work of Caesar's relative, he may have had some private discussion about it; at any rate he removed the *tribuni aerarii* when he came to power himself.

During the consulship of Pompey and Crassus, Caesar was appointed quaestor for 69 for the province of Further Spain. This gave him immediate access to the Senate — one of Sulla's measures that had not been overturned. One of the first recorded actions of Caesar in the Senate is his speech in favour of Pompey's bill to grant an amnesty to the followers of Lepidus and Sertorius. Not that Caesar was totally impartial, since he had in mind his wife's brother Lucius Cinna, who could return from exile if the bill went through.

Just before he was due to depart for Spain, there were two deaths in Caesar's family. His aunt Julia died, and he lost his wife Cornelia. He pronounced a splendid oration at his aunt's funeral. Since she was the widow of Gaius Marius, whose last acts had been among the bloodiest that Rome had seen so far, Caesar was presented with a dilemma. Sulla had forbidden the display of any images of Marius or anything to do with him. Caesar ignored the ban; after all Sulla had been dead for a

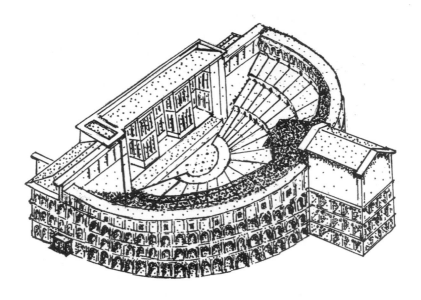

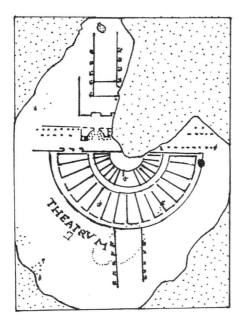

3   Reconstruction drawing of Pompey's theatre. Pompey was the most important man in Rome in the 70s and 60s BC, so this was a political statement as well as an architectural wonder. It was the largest building complex that had ever been erected in Rome up to the time of Pompey the Great, and it was the first permanent theatre. Shows and games had always been held in temporary premises specially built for the purpose and then demolished, but Pompey had seen theatres in the Greek east, especially the one at Mytilene. He was determined to build one in Rome, but opposition to his plan centred around the scandalous reputation of theatrical performances, so Pompey built a huge complex of buildings, with a theatre attached. There was a temple and colonnaded walk, and meeting rooms, in one of which the Senate was convened on the fateful Ides of March. The plan of the theatre is taken from the Forma Urbis, *the marble plan of Rome that was drawn up in Severan times; it survives in fragments, but fortunately almost the whole of the theatre is depicted on one fragment.* Drawn by Jaqui Taylor decade and there was no powerful group in Rome clamouring for the return of his legislation. Sulla's legislation hardly counted for anything now; it was the social and political scene that could make or break. The choice in the current situation was clear: either Caesar whispered a short speech for his aunt Julia, displayed no images of her husband, and hastened the funeral in the hope that if he got it over with quickly no one would notice; or he did it properly. It would give the Roman senators and the people far too much fuel to use against him if he could be accused of trying to cover up his origins, because there would be many a helpful soul willing to shout it from the rooftops, and then it would look as though he was ashamed and frightened to acknowledge his direct connection with Marius. So the alternative was to make a lot of fuss, shout from the rooftops himself to pre-empt anyone else, and give his aunt the most splendid funeral that Rome had ever seen. The same applied when his wife Cornelia died, about the same time. She was the daughter of Cinna, and Caesar was not about to try to cover up her origins either. He gave her a public funeral too, unprecedented because relatively young Roman matrons did not received this honour. Apart from any love and respect that Caesar felt for his aunt and his wife, he was also making a loud political statement for himself.

The two provinces of Hither and Further Spain (*Hispania Citerior* and *Ulterior*) had been annexed by the Romans in 197. There remained large areas of what is now modern Spain where neither Roman conquest nor colonisation had penetrated, but the areas marked out as provinces had attracted many Roman settlers and businessmen. This appointment offered Caesar opportunities to gain experience and also some personal profit. As quaestor he was responsible for pronouncing judgements in the courts, and though he was still small fry on the greater Roman political scene, he was all-important to some provincials. He could make friends and allies in the province, all of whom might come in useful later in his career. Next to nothing is recorded of what he did while he was quaestor, and some sources state that he left before his tour of duty had officially ended, in order to cultivate the Transpadane Gauls with promises that he would try to gain full Roman citizenship for them, since they had received only Latin rights after the Social War. There may be some confusion with his later appointment as governor of Further Spain, when he definitely departed early, but it is not an important factor in his career to establish precisely when he returned to Rome in 68.

Once in Rome, he married again, this time to Pompeia, no relative of Pompey, but the granddaughter of both Quintus Pompeius Rufus and of Sulla himself. Having made his unequivocal statement before he left Rome that he maintained his connections with Marius and Cinna, he now made another one that he was not automatically the foe of any relatives of Sulla. His household was now complete again; he had a wife with solid connections, and a young daughter Julia who would by now be about eight years old. His mother Aurelia was still a force in his life, and remained so. Four years later, when he was intent upon becoming Pontifex Maximus, the anecdote that has been handed down is that he told his mother that he would come home as High Priest or not at all; there is no mention of what he told his wife.

Caesar now required another office that would help him on the road to the consulship. It is hardly in doubt that the consulship was his aim from the earliest times, but because his family connections, though noble, were not outstanding, and he had no immense private fortune, Caesar was handicapped and had to start at the bottom. In 67 he was made curator of the Via Appia, one of the earliest roads dating from the fourth century BC. It ran from Rome to Brundisium, the ancient equivalent of a modern motorway linking Rome with the southern coast of Italy and the Mediterranean. *Curatores* were seemingly not assigned to the roads on a regular annual basis, but from time to time, which probably meant that the roads had degenerated badly by the time an official was appointed. The paved roads that are now taken as the hallmark of the Roman Empire were not yet common, so road surfaces were impermanent and maintenance was essential to fill up potholes. It was a post in which Caesar could earn respect and gratitude as well as notice from his superiors if he carried out his duties assiduously. Travellers expected the curator to repair routes where necessary and attend to their proper functioning, such as drainage and the removal of obstacles; without doubt if improvements were made under Caesar as curator, he would advertise the fact by means of inscriptions on milestones, which had been in common usage for about a century, or whatever other facilities were offered. He probably also spent a lot of his own money, over and above any allocation that may have been made to him, and as a result incurred debts that continued to mount until he began to associate with Crassus, who was famous as a money lender. Then, like modern advertisements for credit card companies, he probably raised a loan to pay off all his other loans, except that perhaps Crassus did not offer a facility for one easy monthly payment; he would hold Caesar in his pocket until his investment paid off. In order to repay his creditors, Caesar relied like many another politician upon being able to make a profit from eventually governing a province, in Caesar's case that of Further Spain, to which he was assigned once again, this time as governor, in 61. He could probably not afford to quarrel too deeply with Marcus Licinius Crassus until he could find the means to support himself.

The Roman political scene still revolved around Pompey. In 67 the tribune Aulus Gabinius put forward a bill to create a special command with extreme, indeed unprecedented, authority over the Mediterranean and up to 50 miles inland in all the coastal areas on the periphery, in order to eradicate the pirate menace once and for all. No commander was named in the bill, but everyone knew that Pompey was behind it. He had developed a technique that he was to use again and again in the future, of sitting back while a problem grew worse and worse, not offering his services or any opinion on the matter, and then reluctantly accepting the command or office when it was finally bestowed on him, usually after his agents had done the background work that was necessary to convince people that he knew how to deal with the situation. On this occasion, Caesar was the only senator who spoke in favour of the bill. He had already suffered imprisonment at the hands of the pirates, and had seen how difficult it could be to persuade anyone to assume the authority to punish them when they had been caught. Besides, he may have experienced something of the problems involved in any official operations against the pirates, since he had probably served briefly under the command of Marcus Antonius, whose command was imbued with wide-ranging powers but not nearly wide-ranging enough, and the end result was failure when Antonius was killed or died in post. Penny-pinching ways of dealing with serious situations irked Caesar, who probably voted openly for the grand plan, and tacitly for Pompey as the best man to put it into operation. Whilst his fingers may have itched for the opportunity to conduct the campaign himself, he could not possibly hope to rival Pompey the Great, who for the next few years was at the zenith of his career. Writing two centuries later and with the benefit of hindsight, Dio says that Caesar voted for the Gabinian law because he foresaw that he might need something similar for himself one day. This cannot be the truth or the whole truth, and most likely Caesar could see that without some such tremendous effort with appropriate powers, cash, ships and men, then good money and good generals would continue to be poured after bad while Rome nibbled away ineffectively at the problem.

The Gabinian law was passed despite opposition from the right-wing senatorial party led by Quintus Lutatius Catulus. Gabinius deposed the tribune Trebellius who tried to veto his proposal, revealing that the restoration of the tribunate had not benefited the populace at all; it had achieved nothing except to perpetuate the use of the office as a mouthpiece for the strongest men in Rome, whoever they were. The Senate may have been opposed to the special command, but the people, who saw in it an end to food shortages caused by piratical disruption of supplies, were firm in their support of it. Caesar's lone voice in favour of the bill from the very beginning will have done him no harm at all in the eyes of the people of Rome, and it had the advantage of bringing him to the notice of Pompey himself, who cannot have failed to note the name of Gaius Julius Caesar as a potential ally. The political reality in 67 may have been distorted by later events; Caesar was destined to outshine Pompey and all other Roman generals, but that was not necessarily apparent before his consulship. His ambition may have been patently obvious to anyone except the most out of touch, but he simply did not have the stature to stand on his own merits. Reality was Pompey, and in the end it was necessary to be either for him or against him. Caesar had decided on the former course.

Pompey leapt into action as soon as another law was passed naming him as the commander against the pirates. He divided the Mediterranean and the coasts into 13 regions and placed a squadron of ships in each; when he embarked for the first assault he was told that it was not propitious to set sail at that moment, but he swept aside all opposition with the bold observation 'It is necessary to sail; it is not necessary to live'. If his ship had foundered, of course, the adjective 'bold' would have been replaced with 'reckless' or 'misguided'. But Pompey was sure of himself and determined. Within about two months, the seas were clear of pirates, who had been resolutely netted up and herded to the coasts of Cilicia. Instead of executing them all, Pompey settled his defeated captives in the coastal cities they had ruined. Now he needed another command.

The war in the east against Mithridates had started well under the command of Lucius Licinius Lucullus. He had forced Mithridates to leave all occupied territories and to take refuge in Armenia, and he had ironed out many abuses against the provincials in an attempt to clean up the dreadful exploitation that had been normal since Sulla's campaigns. He was ready to annexe Pontus, the kingdom of Mithridates, having captured its cities without allowing his soldiers to ransack them. The lack of booty disgruntled the soldiers, who eventually mutinied when Lucullus led them into the highlands of Armenia. They had helped him to win a great battle against Tigranes, the king of Armenia, who had allied, or been coerced into an alliance, with his refugee-guest Mithridates. As a reward, Lucullus allowed the soldiers free rein after they had captured the capital city of Tigranocerta. But Lucullus is generally agreed to have lacked the brilliant touch that Pompey or Caesar had with their armies. In the highlands of Armenia, where perhaps the soldiers could no longer see the point of what they were fighting for, they mutinied. By political means at Rome, Lucullus was gradually deprived of his command; Gabinius finished the process in 67. This meant that the army in the east required a commander, and there just happened to be one in the vicinity who was rounding off a successful campaign against the pirates and would be free to assume command almost at once. The tribune Gaius Manilius had little trouble in passing his law to bestow the command on Pompey in 66. The commander was to have control of all the provinces in Asia Minor, essential if he was to conduct the war properly. He would need supplies from a large area, and he may be forced to chase Mithridates and Tigranes from kingdom to kingdom, through several different provinces. The protocol of crossing boundaries between provinces would have to be waived. He would have the power to make war on other enemies if necessary, and to make treaties. Caesar voted in favour of this law, as did Cicero, who was praetor in 66. For the time being Pompey would be absent in the east, earning fame and fortune for himself. No one could predict when he would return, nor in what capacity or mood. In the meantime, Caesar concentrated on building up his own influence in Rome. When Pompey came back, he would be the man of the moment, eclipsing everyone else; he might be cultivated as a patron for Caesar, but it would be much better to be in a position of relative independence.

Caesar was curule aedile in 65, with Marcus Calpurnius Bibulus as his colleague. The two were fated to run parallel in more than one post, with Bibulus the loser every time. As aediles they were responsible for policing of the streets and markets in Rome, and for the upkeep of temples and public buildings. There would be a kernel of experienced staff for this work already in place, and there was perhaps an allocation of money from public funds to help with expenses, but holders of these posts were expected to contribute from their own pockets, especially to finance the games and shows that they were under obligation to put on. Bibulus made contributions but was never acknowledged because all the credit went to Caesar, who had the charm and charisma and the ability to sell himself to the public that Bibulus never developed. Caesar arranged gladiatorial combats in honour of his late father, and then put out on display all Marius' trophies from his wars. It was a means to an end of becoming well known for generosity and extravagant display. He needed popular favour, especially as dark rumours started to circulate about his possible involvement in the so-called first conspiracy of Catiline. No one will ever know to what extent Caesar was implicated in this abortive plot, nor in the next one that was ended by Cicero in his first and only consulship in 63.

Lucius Sergius Catilina, better known as Catiline, was accused of various crimes including extortion while he was governor of Africa, but no one was able to bring him to book. Prosecutions were arranged but he emerged almost unscathed each time, not that anyone truly believed in his innocence, but happily for him, firm evidence of what he was up to was simply not available. In 65 the consuls elect, Publius Autronius and Publius Sulla, were disqualified on the charge of corruption in their election campaign, and Lucius Aurelius Cotta and Lucius Manlius Torquatus were elected instead. It was alleged that the disappointed candidates contacted Catiline, and it is further alleged that they plotted together to assassinate the appointed consuls at the beginning of the year, and then presumably they were going to take over the state. If such was the case, the plot failed. The story is smoke without fire, rumour made pseudo-fact. No one can even be sure that there was a plot, and if there were, it is still doubtful whether Catiline was involved in it. Cicero, who wrote about these events in a contemporary pamphlet called *de Consiliis Suis* (it was not published until after his death) is certain of the existence of some shady dealings, but he does not mention any involvement of Caesar in this first conspiracy. He did think that Crassus was implicated, however, and if Crassus was involved then it might follow that Caesar at least knew of the plot. It has been argued that stories of his complicity have been invented after he rose to power and maliciously backdated. Rumours circulated that Crassus was going to make himself Dictator in the ensuing mayhem after Catiline's plot, and Caesar was to be his master of horse (*magister equitum*). In that case it might seem that Catiline was to be used to stir up trouble that Crassus and Caesar could then heroically stamp out. The situation is even more nebulous now than it was at the time, but it does demonstrate that the association of Crassus and Caesar was considered to be strong and their joint ambition unbounded. This perception may have been retrospective, and even if it were contemporary it does not necessarily have any basis in fact. But it may not have been considered damaging. It may even have been a perception that both Crassus and Caesar would have revelled in. Fear of the worst makes acceptance of a less fearsome proposal so much the easier.

Other stories were told of their mutual scheming in 65. Crassus was censor in that year with Quintus Lutatius Catulus as his colleague. Catulus had spoken against Gabinius' and Manilius' bills to bestow the special commands on Pompey. He was a devout follower of Sulla, and had given him a state funeral; he had done most to put down Lepidus' ill-judged rebellion. He stood for everything that was conservative and was the antithesis of men like Caesar. The duties of the censors were to compile the lists of Roman citizens and to review the membership of the Senate with a view to ousting any who were considered unsuitable, or electing those who were worthy. Crassus tried to put into practice Caesar's promise of full citizenship to the Transpadane Gauls. Catulus blocked him. He also blocked the proposal to annexe Egypt as a Roman province, a real possibility since the ruler set up by Sulla in 80, Ptolemy XI Alexander, had been murdered after a very short reign, but he had allegedly left a will that would have bequeathed the kingdom to Rome, just as Attalus of Pergamum had done in 133. It could be said that Ptolemy Alexander's successor, Ptolemy XII nicknamed Auletes (the

4 *Bust of Marcus Tullius Cicero. It is through Cicero's letters to his friends, principally Atticus, that we have an intimate portrait of Caesar from close quarters. The two opposed each other in 63 when the consul Cicero executed the Catilinarian conspirators, and Caesar as a rising politician spoke against the execution.* Photo courtesy of the Victoria and Albert Museum

fluteplayer), had no legal claim to the throne of Egypt. Roman interest in Egypt was of long ancestry, and sprang from only one cause: it was the wealthiest land in the world. Given that Caesar did not actually annexe it when he had the opportunity after the battle of Pharsalus, but instead set up Cleopatra as its Queen, there may be some soupçon of doubt about the story that he hoped to be given the command of Egypt in order to put into operation the terms of Ptolemy XI Alexander's will.

All Crassus' proposals during his term as censor were defeated by Catulus, so the Egyptian adventure came to nothing. The following two years were even more fraught. Catiline refused to be discouraged at his lack of political success. He had been defeated in the consular elections in 66, and had been unable to stand as a candidate in 65 and 64 because he had been undergoing prosecutions at the time, but had not been condemned. He had friends in high places; several aristocrats, including ex consulars, spoke favourably of him — not that this is any recommendation of good character, only of solidarity with his peers. But it is likely that his reputation has been blackened retrospectively after he had raised revolt and then been defeated; it is a normal human process to disassociate oneself from the condemned, pretending that one had great discernment but kept silent at the time: 'Well, I never liked him, of course'. Now he made it known that he desired the consulship for 63, so he started to agitate in the run up to the elections. There were only three candidates, and still Catiline failed to be elected; Gaius Antonius Hybrida, an uncle of Mark Antony, and Marcus Tullius Cicero were to be the consuls of 63. Catiline bided his time; he could try again next year.

At the end of 64 the tribune Publius Servilius Rullus entered upon office on the traditional date of 10 December. He introduced a land bill in the early part of 63 that has been repeatedly discussed and disputed by modern scholars. It was never put into effect, so discussion is perhaps somewhat academic, but its failure may have inflamed those who had hoped to gain from it, and thereby served to provide Catiline with a band of discontents in Rome and Italy. Rullus' bill would have solved several problems at once, and a lot of thought had gone into the preparation of its clauses. Rullus attempted to satisfy many needs while also treading carefully between forced sales or seizures of lands, both public and private, and he wanted to avoid making insufficient allocations for the needy. The urban poor were to be given lands, which would dramatically reduce their numbers in the city of Rome and therefore also reduce the potential riots because of food shortages. The soldiers settled by Sulla were to be left unmolested, unless they expressed a wish to sell their lands. The provinces were to be included in the allotments, but only where land could be purchased by the state. There was to be a commission of ten men, each with the powers of a praetor for five years, with a staff of administrators and secretaries. They were not to be responsible to anyone, so the land commissioners could not be harassed by rising or established politicians, and there could be no question of any predominant personal interest. Cicero as consul bludgeoned the bill to an early death. He sold it to the populace as a scam, protesting that the allocations of lands would be worthless, consisting of marshes or swamps, and that selling public lands would entail loss of revenues to the state. Chiefly he was protesting on behalf of Pompey who would require land for his veterans when he returned home, which might be quite soon; the argument ran that the commission of ten excluded Pompey or any of his representatives, and so it was a blow aimed at him by some anti-Pompeian aristocrats, widely believed to be Crassus and Caesar, trying to build up a power base against him before he came home.

Interpretations of Rullus' land bill diverge into two polarised arguments. Some modern historians follow Cicero's line of reasoning that the plan was to embarrass Pompey, and could therefore have been a ploy on the part of Crassus and Caesar to hold him to ransom when he returned, needing above all else land for his soldiers. Others, notably Gruen, argue that on the contrary the bill was designed to assist Pompey, as its timing reveals, by preparing for a properly-organised system just as the veterans of the Mithridatic war were due to return. The evidence is not detailed enough to refute either argument, and so any resolution depends, like much else about this period, on opinion.

Whatever his stance on Rullus' bill, Caesar was beginning to make a name for himself in 63. He prosecuted Gaius Calpurnius Piso, because he had executed a Transpadane Gaul. He had taken the Transpadanes under his wing, and though they had not received the citizenship that he had promised them, thanks to the opposition of Catulus, Caesar must now keep faith with them in order to preserve his credibility, otherwise it would seem that he was simply toying with any device that might bring him fame. Piso was acquitted, but Caesar had made his statement; he would not be blamed for his failure when it was clear that the nobility of Rome closed ranks against outsiders. He also defended a Numidian nobleman in a case against king Hiempsal, who was attempting to reduce the chief and his people to the status of vassals. Caesar stood for justice for the oppressed, and as far as possible he kept his promises.

In the notorious trial of the aged Gaius Rabirius, who had killed the tribune Saturninus nearly forty years earlier, Caesar acted in collusion with Titus Labienus, one of the tribunes in 63. Tribunes were theoretically sacrosanct, no matter how unscrupulous they had been, so the murder of Saturninus was a terrible crime; it was not the last time that Caesar would place great emphasis on the sacrosanctity of tribunes. In reality, the attack was not directed solely at Rabirius, but at the workings of the Senate who had passed the *senatus consultum ultimum* when the crisis over the actions of Saturninus and Glaucia came to a head. Caesar was nominated as judge, and gave the death sentence. Rabirius probably appealed to the people; at any rate he was not put to death, but defended by both Cicero and Hortensius. Perhaps Caesar never intended the case to be anything but a show of strength, since the trial was ended by the antiquated method of lowering the flag on the Janiculum hill, a procedure which in Rome's past meant that the city was about to be attacked, thus terminating any business. It was the praetor Quintus Caecilius Metelleus Celer who ordered the flag to be lowered, and many historians are of the opinion that this was prearranged between Caesar and Metellus, especially since the trial was not resumed.

The most important step that Caesar took in 63 was to stand for election as Pontifex Maximus. This office was bestowed for life, and the postholder Metellus Pius died in 64. It was to be expected that an older, more experienced man should be successful, so Catulus probably thought that he was bound to be elected, until he learned that Caesar's accomplice Labienus was to propose that voting should be returned to the people, as had been the custom in the past. This would mean that Caesar's money would speak more loudly and find the right targets. Catulus tried to buy him off, but Caesar was not interested in money. He wanted the supreme priestly office for its political influence. And he was elected. The world may have heard no more of him had he been unsuccessful, since he told his mother that he would return home as Pontifex Maximus or not at all, though it might seem uncharacteristically melodramatic to go off somewhere and commit suicide in the event of failure. He meant that he was sure of victory; and if by some quirk of fate he had been foiled he would have thought of something else.

Towards the end of the year the famous Catilinarian conspiracy was revealed by the consul Cicero's vigilant investigations. During the year 63 Catiline had been defeated in the elections for the third time, in his attempt to become consul for 62. It may have been only at this moment that he hatched a plot in a monumental fit of pique, frustrated that power and influence, and the means to repay his debts were denied him yet again. It was unlikely that he would be any more successful in subsequent elections, and in any case he did not wish to wait for another year. There were plenty of men in Rome who bore any number of grudges or who shared similar frustrations. The promise of land had been dangled before the urban poor and then obliterated when Rullus' bill came to nothing. There were some senators whose careers had been blighted, and who found association with Catiline an attractive proposition. One of them was Publius Cornelius Lentulus Sura. He had been consul in 71, but had fallen foul of Pompey and his party, and had been removed from the Senate by the censors during the consulship of Pompey and Crassus in 70. After reaching the consulship, Lentulus had to embark on a second career from the beginning. He was to be unwittingly instrumental in bringing the conspiracy to a sudden head, giving Cicero all the evidence he needed to arrest him and his accomplices. He had the further distinction of having married Julia, the widow of Marcus Antonius and the mother of three boys, the eldest of whom was Mark Antony. Cicero's treatment of Lentulus Sura made an enemy of the young Antony.

Catiline's following was not overwhelmingly numerous, and comprised a cross-section of Roman society, rich and poor alike, all those who could be persuaded to follow an aristocrat who promised reforms, cancellation of debts, redistribution of wealth, and in short, a better world. The surviving accounts of the rebellion, by Cicero and Sallust, are hostile. Cicero had a vested interest in portraying Catiline as a thoroughly unprincipled villain, so that his brave stance against him would seem all the more worthy. Sallust wrote the *Bellum Catilinae*, or *de Catilinae Coniuratione*, nearly two decades later, when he was firmly in Caesar's camp, so although he accepts Cicero's portrayal, he plays down the consul's achievements and writes at length about the contributions of Caesar and Cato, contrasting their completely opposite opinions. There is no voice, contemporary or later, from Catiline's side of the affair that might explain what he was trying to achieve.

At the end of October it seems that Catiline planned to begin an armed rebellion outside Rome, and to assassinate the consuls and other senators, but the assassinations failed, or were foiled. As yet Cicero had not enough incontrovertible evidence to persuade the whole Senate to act, but by mid-November Catiline joined the army in Etruria, and was declared *hostis*, or a public enemy. In December the Catilinarians made a fatal mistake; Lentulus Sura and other senators tried to convert to the Catilinarian cause some Gallic envoys from the tribe of the Allobroges, who were leaving Rome after presenting an unsuccessful petition. It was thought that the Gauls may have been sufficiently discontented to turn against the Roman government, but rather than embroil themselves in a plot, they reported to Cicero. He arrested five ringleaders, including Lentulus Sura. Four more arrests were made shortly afterwards.

It was a tense moment for Caesar and Crassus. They were not accused outright but there was suspicion that they had aided and abetted Catiline, if not instigated the whole plot. Catulus was still bitter after his failure to be elected Pontifex Maximus, and so he agitated to discredit and possibly remove Caesar. There was a debate in the Senate on 5 December to decide the course of action with regard to the first five men who had been arrested. Cicero did not advocate the death penalty as such, but everyone knew what he meant in his speech, and the senior members of the Senate all suggested that it should be adopted. Caesar had won election as praetor for 62 and so was entitled to speak after the consulars. He pleaded for the lives of the Catilinarians by advising that the arrested men should be separated and held in different Italian towns, never to return to Rome. All their property was to be confiscated, and no one was ever to plead for them on pain of being declared an enemy of the state. He could not plead for acquittal, because that would make it seem more obvious than ever that he was somehow implicated in the plot, and at the same time he could not plead too vociferously for the death penalty, because that would make it seem as though he was anxious to destroy the evidence by removing men who could testify against him. So he trod the middle path, suggested a lifelong punishment of considerable severity, and rounded off his speech with the warning that there would be repercussions later if the death penalty were passed without giving the accused the benefit of a trial. He had been instrumental in prosecuting Rabirius four decades after the murder of Saturninus, so he had strong reason to warn Cicero not to act too hastily.

But Cicero was a lawyer, and he knew how a proper trial could be dragged out, and how defence lawyers could work up a good case, and the result might be acquittal. Furthermore, his consulship was nearing its end, and it would be an anti-climax to exit from his term of office having revealed the plot without having decisively saved the state. He wanted drama and heroics. There was a new voice in the Senate, one that helped him to bring the proceedings to a speedy and bloody end. Marcus Porcius Cato had embarked on his career as quaestor in the previous year, and so he could pass an opinion when his turn came to speak. He was very good at it, and from 63 onwards he scarcely ever stopped speaking, consistently in opposition to Caesar. By suggesting an alternative punishment to the death sentence Caesar had almost swayed the Senate to his point of view, but Cato whipped it back into line. He proposed the death penalty, and the vote went his way. The five Catilinarians, including Mark Antony's stepfather Lentulus Sura, were executed immediately. Cicero was to pay a high price for his victory.

Though the ringleaders had been captured, Catiline was still free, with an army behind him. The consul Gaius Antonius was sent against him but he suffered an attack of gout and withdrew. The senatorial army prevailed in the end; indeed, by the time the battles were fought Catiline's men had dwindled to such small proportions that defeat could only be postponed, not avoided. Before it was clear that there was no further danger from Catiline, the tribune Metellus Nepos, one of Pompey's men who had been released from military service in the east in order to represent his commander in Rome, proposed that Pompey should be recalled to save the state from the conspirators. Cato blocked the proposal by fine if long-winded oratory, just as he opposed the proposal to allow Pompey to stand for the consulship *in absentia*. Caesar was praetor, and supported Metellus when he came to read out the bill on the steps of the temple of Castor and Pollux. But the tribune Cato and his colleague Minucius Thermus seated themselves between Caesar and Nepos, and vetoed the bill. This staunch attitude met with violence, mostly orchestrated by Nepos, and Cato was subjected to a fierce stoning in the Forum, but being a Stoic he bore it, stoically, and eventually won the day. Nepos went back to the east, unable to achieve anything for Pompey. Caesar had already been forbidden to exercise the functions as praetor, and now closeted himself in his house, dismissing his lictors who

5   *Bust of Marcus Porcius Cato found at Volubilis in North Africa. Caesar's constant enemy, Cato resolutely opposed any unorthodox political schemes, but on one occasion even Cicero accused him of being unrealistic. At the end of his life, when he rallied and united the defeated Pompeians in Africa, he gained in prestige; he earned the admiration of the people of Utica for his judgement and consideration as governor. He committed suicide when Caesar was finally victorious at Thapsus, and as a consequence of this martyrdom he became an even more powerful enemy of Caesar than he had ever been while alive.* Rabat Museum; photo David Brearley

walked in front of officials carrying the rods and axes, symbols of Roman power. The first indication that he had a following among the populace is revealed now, because the mob threatened to riot if he was not reinstated. It is unlikely that this was a spontaneous demonstration of the will of the people on behalf of a praetor they knew and liked. Caesar knew how to pull whatever strings were necessary and had by now built up good contacts. He was soon back in office.

His duties were mainly legal, and in the aftermath of the conspiracy of Catiline he fought a rearguard action against men who were ready to accuse him of complicity in the plot. Two men, Quintus Curius and Lucius Vettius, both alleged that Caesar had written to Catiline, and promised to produce a letter that would condemn him. Caesar reacted fast and furiously. He defended himself to the Senate, protesting that he had revealed information to Cicero and had nothing to hide. He meted out violent punishment to Vettius, and as further good measure he also punished Novius Niger, the president of one of the courts, because he was the man to whom Vettius had brought his allegations. These measures discouraged any further attacks on him. Whether or not he had any part in the conspiracy of Catiline must remain conjectural. He was distrusted, but no one could find solid evidence, and in any case it must be asked what he could have achieved by joining Catiline. There were several senators of noble rank and considerable experience in Catiline's following, who would be first in the queue for high offices. Caesar would have been one of many, and that was simply not his style. Caesar wanted to be one and only, not part of a group. When he was setting out for Spain as governor in 61, his route took him through a village, and he remarked that he would rather be the first man in that small settlement rather than the second man in Rome. He may never have made this remark, but whoever invented it for him was not too wide of the mark in assessing him. If he joined the conspiracy of Catiline at all it will have been with the aim of eventually leading it and shaping events, or turning against it to squash it. Cancellation of debts, one of the items on Catiline's agenda, would have helped him but he would not risk everything simply on that count.

His debts were legendary, so when he was allocated Further Spain as his province as his praetorship ended he will have immediately sought for a means of garnering wealth to pay all that he owed and to assemble the fortune he would need to finance the next stage in his career. Before he left for his province, his household was the subject of a scandal. As Pontifex Maximus, the festival of the Bona Dea was held at his residence, presided over by the women of his immediate family, in this case his wife and mother. Only women were allowed to attend, but this time the ceremony was interrupted by the quaestor elect Publius Clodius Pulcher, for reasons which have never been properly elucidated. Perhaps it was simply a prank when he dressed as a woman and tried to join in. Aurelia discovered him, and threw him out. Without waiting to find out if Clodius was having an affair with his wife, Caesar divorced Pompeia, because, as he said, Caesar's wife must be above suspicion. If he suffered from any vacillation or emotional outbursts, nothing has been recorded. He was resolute, decisive and ruthless when it came to his reputation and his political and social standing. His position as Pontifex Maximus ought not to be compromised, and as he was about to depart for Spain, where he would remain for at least a year, he would not wish to put temptation in Clodius' way, or in the way of Pompeia. His household would be looked after by his mother in his absence.

6 *Map of the Roman Empire at the time of Caesar. Provinces had been acquired in east and west, the latest additions made by Pompey after his eastern campaigns. The term province originally described a task to be fulfilled, and did not necessarily refer to a territory. Some of the retiring magistrates of Rome took up a pro-magistracy after their term of office, which could involve special tasks such as attending to the food supply, or the administration of roads or forests. Gradually as Rome acquired more territories, the pro-magistrates were assigned to a province, i.e. a tour of duty as governor of one of the new territories. Hence the word province was eventually applied to the territory itself. The Province in Caesar's day referred to the area of southern Gaul around Massilia and Narbo. The old name survives as Provence, despite the fact that the province was also known as Transalpine Gaul, and then Gallia Narbonensis. The first Gallic province protected the route into Spain, not all of which was yet conquered.* Drawn by Jan Shearsmith

He left Rome as Pompey returned from the east, and in the same year Clodius was prosecuted for his sacrilege in disrupting the ceremony of the Bona Dea. Both events were to have cumulative consequences. Pompey refused to emulate Sulla by marching on Rome, and though he had expressed a wish to stand for the consulship *in absentia*, he did not force his way to the elections when he was refused permission by the Senate. He disbanded his army and entered Rome as conquering hero, but not conquering tyrant. His triumph in the autumn was splendid. Undoubtedly successful as a general, political success was denied him. He had won bigger and better victories than any Roman before him and enriched the city on a scale unheard of after even the most brilliant campaigns. He had been thwarted of his wish to stand for the consulship, but he still had an unassailable reputation and a wide circle of agents and clients. His influence ought to have been preponderant, and he could have expected that the settlement of his veterans and the ratification of his arrangements for the eastern provinces would be a brief formality. But the climate in Rome had changed; the aristocrats had gathered strength and a few of the leading members closed ranks against him. His main opponent was Lucullus, still smarting under the humiliation of being wrested from the eastern command and then watching from Rome as Pompey went from victory to victory. Now he persuaded the Senate that Pompey's settlement of the east should be dissected clause by clause. Cato supported him, using his particular talents for talking ideas to death in debates. This was the situation as Caesar entered his province.

As governor of Further Spain, he was entitled to funds from the public treasury, but he did not wait for any funds to be voted to him. It was said he was fleeing from his creditors. Crassus paid all his bills for him, but on what terms is uncertain. Once in Spain, Caesar embarked upon a campaign against the lawless bandits of Lusitania. According to Plutarch he had 20 cohorts at his disposal and raised ten more, presumably from Spanish natives. Then he set the scene for his aggressive action against the brigands. He ordered them to come out of their mountain strongholds and settle in the lower-lying areas in peace and quiet. He would probably have been most disconcerted if the bandits had done just that, but fortunately for his plans they refused, giving him the excuse that he needed to round them up and defeat them. Some diehards fled to an island off the west coast of Spain, where they managed to repel Caesar's attempted landing from rafts. After a short delay Caesar brought ships from Gades (modern Cadiz) and captured all the bandits. He followed up his victory with a display of naval and military strength to other cities, notably Brigantium on the northern coast. By means of these exploits he filled his own coffers, carefully sent some of the proceeds to Rome, and sensibly allowed the soldiers under his command to share the booty. The bandits had presumably hoarded a ready supply of goods stolen from somebody else. Back in Rome Caesar was accused of sacking places that had submitted to him peacefully, but there was no trial, and no mention of extortion; he cannot be accused of exploitation of the Spanish provincials. This does not mean to say that he was averse to accepting gifts, and there would be many of those from grateful men and women who appreciated his activities in suppressing bandits, bringing peace to the settled areas, hearing cases in court, and so on. There would also be gifts from people who hoped

7   *Map of the eastern Mediterranean and the surrounding provinces where Caesar fought his first battles.* Drawn by Jan Shearsmith

to be grateful in the future. He tried to rectify problems that were brought to him from the provincials, who were still emerging from the aftermath of the war against Sertorius. As a patron Caesar was loyal and supportive; no doubt he chose carefully before engaging in any kind of relationship.

One important contact from Spain was Lucius Cornelius Balbus from Gades. Though Balbus was originally a protégé of Pompey, to whom he owed his Roman citizenship, his allegiance was transferred to Caesar, who benefited greatly as quaestor and then governor in Spain from his association with him. Balbus was extremely wealthy, a factor that probably had a bearing on the association, at least from Caesar's point of view. In these early days it may have been clear to Balbus that Caesar was destined for greater things and could help him to rise too, but that was subject to chance, and in the circumstances of the time during the late sixties, Caesar might never be able to step from under Pompey's shadow.

After pacifying the bandit-infested country and attending to civil government of the province, Caesar turned his full attention to Rome. He left before his successor had arrived, intent on the election campaign for the consulship of 59. He was voted a triumph for his achievements in pacifying the Lusitanian bandits, but he faced a dilemma. If he wanted to hold the triumph he must remain outside Rome, or forfeit his command (*imperium*) if he entered the city. But if he wanted to stand for the consulship he had to present himself in person in Rome. Pompey had been refused permission to stand *in absentia*, so it was unlikely that the Senate would reverse its decisions in Caesar's favour. The Senate had gone even further to thwart him in his future career after his consulship. Anticipating that he might become consul, the Senate made sure that there was no territorial province to be assigned to the consuls of 59 after their terms of office ended, but the main responsibility was to be the care of the woodlands and paths, which is closer to the term in its original sense; province originally meant a duty of any description, and did not necessarily denote a territory.

This lowly duty for the retiring consuls of 59 was meant to be the Senate's safeguard if Caesar did become consul, since the senators had probably guessed correctly that he would abandon the triumph in search of a better goal. So the only senatorial gain that had been achieved so far was to prevent Caesar from holding his triumph and advertising his talents to the people of Rome. It was not much of a victory, all things considered. The intransigence of the Senate in opposing Pompey and frustrating his wishes, and in churlishly making Caesar choose between pomp and circumstance and real power, merely set the stage for a momentous year and the Senate's humiliation in 59. The election of Caesar as consul was a foregone conclusion as soon as he entered Rome.

3 The consulship of Julius and Caesar

The new consul had already established a reputation as a clever and somewhat dangerous politician. His ultimate achievements, glorious or infamous depending on one's point of view, obscure his early career because it is virtually impossible to cast off knowledge of the outcome when dealing with each stage of Caesar's life. Contemporary opinion unaltered by hindsight is not abundant. Only the works of Cicero can elucidate in any depth how Caesar was perceived before he became Dictator, and even then this evidence represents the views of only a very narrow cross-section of his colleagues, if not an entirely individual outlook. Before Caesar's consulship began, Cicero wrote to his friend Atticus that he hoped that Caesar's policies could be modified, so he feared disruption, but he was probably unable to predict the details of those policies and just how the disruption would make itself felt. It was fairly obvious that Caesar would introduce a new land bill, and there were a number of loose ends still not tied up since the return of Pompey from the east, so it was probably clear to contemporaries that there would be some kind of wheeling and dealing between the two of them. All Pompey's efforts to install his own candidates in significant offices had come to nothing. His supporters Marcus Pupius Piso, who was consul in 61, and Lucius Afranius, consul the following year, were ineffective, and the tribune Flavius had introduced a land bill that met with the usual intransigence and defeat. The result was that the settlement of Pompey's veteran soldiers and the ratification of his eastern conquests seemed as far away in 59 as they had been in 61.

Here was a cause that Caesar could take up in his consulship. No one knows who made the first overtures to whom, but collusion there must have been. Contemporaries may not have realised what was happening until Caesar began to introduce his legislation. If there were rumours, it may have seemed to some that an alliance was impossible. Since Caesar and Crassus had already formed an unofficial partnership largely based on give and take (Crassus gave, Caesar took), and since there was no love lost between Crassus and Pompey, it might have seemed that one would act as a counterweight to the other, perhaps even neutralising Caesar's achievements. Despite Sulla's infamous example and a few little studiously innocent demonstrations by Pompey, this was not yet the era when political issues were routinely decided by the presence of troops, so the avenues open to Caesar lay with either the Senate and/or the people, and with whatever means he could find to adapt political processes as far as they would bend.

Modern historians have labelled the partnership of Caesar, Pompey and Crassus the First Triumvirate, a title that helps to elucidate the course of Roman history but is misleading because it imbues the alliance of three with a permanence and an officially recognised political organisation that it did not possess. The coalition in 59 was limited to the achievement of certain goals, and there it might have ended with each partner going their separate ways, but it was renewed and strengthened in 56 when the three met for what is now termed the conference at Luca (modern Lucca). The so-called Second Triumvirate, the alliance between Caesar's great nephew Octavian, Mark Antony and Lepidus, closely paralleled this syndicate of Caesar, Pompey and Crassus, in that in each case three men worked together to meet their own immediate aims and to direct the course of the state towards those aims. But there was one important difference. Caesar's alliance with Pompey and Crassus was private, unofficial, and unauthorised. By contrast, Octavian, Antony and Lepidus were very careful to have their alliance officially recognised, sanctified even, by law. The three men operated under the title *IIIviri rei publicae constituendae*, literally three men with the power to reconstruct the state. They were granted powers equal to the consuls for a term of five years. This gave them a tremendous advantage that Caesar did not have. He was not blessed with mutually minded consular colleagues in office during 59, and he had only one year instead of five in which to push through a great deal of legislation, if possible by ordinary, traditional means.

One group in the Senate recognised quite early that Caesar as consul represented a challenge if not a threat. Marcus Porcius Cato, traditionalist with a capital T, upright member of the Senate, confirmed Stoic and stickler for the right way of doing things, would normally have abhorred bribery and corruption in order to secure the election of a consular candidate, but he sanctioned it now to have his son-in-law Marcus Calpurnius Bibulus elected. One point in Cato's favour was that bribery had become so widespread in electioneering that by now it could almost be described as traditional. But the charge of hypocrisy is the kindest way of describing Cato's and Bibulus' attitudes. The most commonly used adjective applied to Bibulus, in modern works, is 'unfortunate'. He knew Caesar from their term of office as aediles, when Caesar stole all the credit that was to be had, because he had a much more developed instinct for self-advertisement. As consul, Bibulus fared no better.

Caesar came to the consulship with a ready-made agenda. It included several pressing items: a land bill that would accommodate the settlement of Pompey's veterans and perhaps alleviate the population pressures in Rome; the ratification of the eastern provinces and client kingdoms that Pompey had made before he returned home; sorting out the Asian tax collectors' bids which had gone awry; the reform of the law to attempt once again to curb extortionate practices of provincial governors. For Caesar's own purposes, he required a provincial command that would bring military glory and booty, rather than the administration of forests and pathways that the Senate had allocated to the outgoing consuls of 59. Finally he needed to install a few candidates in official posts for 58 and subsequent years, and to establish a mechanism to ensure the survival of his legislation that would no doubt be attacked as soon as he left Rome.

The land bill was the most urgent, and where other land bills had failed on certain points Caesar doctored his bill until it ironed out all the problems. There were to be no compulsory purchases of land, so only the men who wished to sell would be approached. This meant that the earlier settlements of Sulla's veterans and others would not be disrupted, and no one should feel under threat of expulsion. It denied any chance for Caesar's opponents to take up the cause of unjustly evicted farmers, because there were to be none who could wave banners, adding to the urban mass in Rome. Indeed the bill when fully operative would relieve population pressure by providing land for the poor so they could move out. Priority was to be given to Pompey's veterans, but there would still be enough allotments, even though the Campanian lands were not to be touched. The price to be paid for lands where owners were willing to sell was to be related to the last census ratings, and not to any inflated market price that might be snatched out of the air with a view to quick profit. The cash for the purchase of land was already lying in the coffers, thanks to Pompey's eastern conquests, so it was fitting that his veterans should be settled by means of the wealth he had brought to Rome; war could be seen to have paid for war, still with tangible profits to the state. Building upon the experiences of Livius Drusus, Rullus, and Pompey's tribune Flavius, Caesar had thought of everything in his bill. His enemies hated him for it and spoke against it anyway. There was nothing substantial that they could find on which to pin any serious arguments, but discussion went on and on. Cato spoke towards the end of the debate, and talked and talked. And talked. And went on talking. He meant to talk the bill to death that day, and probably in all the days thereafter. He had a fertile mind that could keep the words coming and he obviously possessed the healthiest vocal chords in the Roman world, a worthy rival to the famous Demosthenes. Perhaps he had household slaves following him around with a ready supply of honeyed drinks.

Caesar now made a mistake. Sunset was approaching, and then the whole session would have to be brought to an end, without the favourable conclusion that he had hoped for. The senators would have time to think about each clause of the land bill, and with the echoes of whatever Cato had talked about running round their heads, debate would continue in the next session, each speaker dissecting the bill sentence by sentence, word by word. This is what the Senate had done to Pompey's bill for the settlement of the east, until it ceased to exist. Caesar had no intention of letting this happen; there was so much else he wanted to do in the rest of the year. He had Cato arrested and sent to prison. Perhaps he had overestimated his own popularity, or underestimated Cato's. Many senators followed the prisoner to gaol, because as one of them said, they preferred to be in prison with Cato than in the Senate with Caesar. So Caesar had Cato released and adjourned the session.

Cato was for the moment on the moral high ground. Caesar had been able to show the public that his opponents were unreasonable, but all his political gains were nullified by his arrest of Cato. He had revealed his hand too early and cast a doubtful light on his methods. He had attempted to have his bill passed by the Senate by the usual means, and would continue to try to do everything else by traditional methods, at least at first. Then he resorted to other means, and succeeded in spite of the Senate and his enemies within it. On the whole, he would be able to cast his opponents in the roles of intransigent, uncaring, narrow-minded, selfish oligarchs, but he would never be able to escape entirely from the salient point that they were justified in making, that they abhorred the dominance of one man or of a small junta, however beneficial the advocated policies may have been for the state as a whole, or for the individuals who made up the state. The most exasperating aspect about his opponents from Caesar's point of view was that they laid more emphasis on methods than on purpose or results, and they were reactive rather than proactive. Cato knew very well how to oppose but not how to propose; he blocked unconstructively, without offering an alternative; compromise was not in his vocabulary. He and his party would have opposed men similar to Caesar and policies similar to his, no matter who proposed them, so it cannot be said that they allowed blind hatred of one man to colour their judgement. But in the final analysis it was Caesar who thought in terms of the Roman Empire rather than the city of Rome surrounded by provinces with exploitable resources. Naturally he exploited with the best of them and was extremely good at it, but at the same time he knew when to stop and how to integrate the exploited, and

8 Head of Caesar
   from Egypt,
   carved from
   green slate.
   Courtesy
   Berlin
   Museen

he saw that changes were inevitable if Rome was to expand; she could not continue to utilise the systems devised to govern a small city state to administer her growing Empire. Change is what frightens most people, though they will find all sorts of high-flown reasons for opposing it rather than admitting their fear.

It cannot have taken Caesar and Pompey by surprise that the land bill did not have a smooth passage through the Senate, so presumably when they went on to the next stage it was already planned in advance. There were plenty of Pompey's veterans who could be called upon to demonstrate solidarity in Rome. They and the tribune Publius Vatinius between them made it clear how serious Caesar and Pompey were about the land bill and their other measures. Still trying to act properly, Caesar asked Bibulus to state if he had objections to any of the clauses of the bill, and presumably he asked him to explain what would be necessary to make him change his mind. Instead of producing a list of valid objections, Bibulus refused to compromise or meet Caesar halfway, falling back on his unwillingness to countenance any changes while he was consul. Perhaps unwisely he burst out to the assembled people that they would not get the land bill this year, even if they all wanted it. Caesar was probably overjoyed, because Bibulus' uncooperative dog-in-the-manger attitude was now out in the open. He took his bill to the people, calling an assembly in the Forum. Crassus appeared with him, and Pompey made a speech outlining the benefits of the land settlements. When asked by Caesar what he would do if there was violence from the opponents of the bill, Pompey declared that if anyone opposed it with the sword then he would use both sword and shield. Dramatic stuff, but it cleared the way for the vote. On the day when voting was conducted, Bibulus and his retinue of three tribunes were prevented from approaching the scene; Vatinius' and Pompey's soldiers did their work well, and as anonymously as possible. No source states exactly what happened except in broad detail; Bibulus was dowsed in mire, and possibly nearly killed, but friends saved him from becoming a martyr to the cause by dragging him into a temple. Caesar's land bill became law, and the committee of 20 could be appointed to oversee its operation. Pompey and Crassus were the most eminent members of this committee. All senators had to take an oath to support the law; Cato and some of his die-hard friends held out for a while, but were persuaded by Cicero that there was little to be gained by refusing to take the oath.

Bibulus called a meeting of the Senate the day after the riots at the voting session, probably in the hope that a state of emergency could be declared, and then he could be appointed Dictator. If such was his plan no one supported him eagerly enough to propose the measure, so without backing from the majority of senators he was powerless. There had been support for Cato when he was arrested and there was physical and verbal support for Bibulus when at some unknown date Vatinius tried to imprison him. But it stopped short of granting him special powers to defeat his fellow consul, who had special powers of a different kind, determination being only a part of them. From now onwards Bibulus retired to his house, watching the skies for omens. In theory, this religious ploy meant that no public business could be conducted and in consequence it nullified all Caesar's acts passed while his colleague was gazing at the heavens. But Caesar had his destiny in mind as well as his *dignitas*, so he ignored Bibulus' omens. He still had a lot to do, and the year was passing by.

Next, Pompey's eastern settlements were ratified, this time without the tiresome senatorial debates. Lucullus had a vested interest in hindering Pompey because he had been in command before Pompey took over, and he deserved at least some credit for his battles before he lost the faith of his troops. It is said that he tried to speak against the arrangements for the east, and Caesar rounded on him, threatening to prosecute him for his failures in command. Lucullus then fell on his knees and begged for mercy, an act for which there are various interpretations. It may have been a sign of abject cowardice, or it may have been an ironic gesture, to show that Caesar was the one man to be feared in Rome, that he would stop at nothing to get what he wanted, and soon everyone would be at his mercy.

Caesar pressed on regardless, attending to details. Some time before his consulship, which many people now began to call the consulship of Julius and Caesar, discounting Bibulus altogether, the tax collectors for the province of Asia had put in a bid for the contract, and found themselves embarrassed because the profits were not what they had expected and so their bid was too high. They had to ask the Senate to relent, and Crassus had tried to alleviate the position, but it was Caesar who finally pushed through the necessary legislation, cautioning the tax gatherers not to make the same mistake again. The Egyptian question still required attention. Ptolemy Auletes at last gained official recognition from Rome, though at a price. He was already in debt to Roman money lenders, but he could draw on the seemingly inexhaustible resources of Egypt, especially if he was secure on his throne, endorsed by the power of Rome. Pompey and Caesar made fortunes out of the arrangement, and the scene was set for the final act of the civil war, when Pompey went to Egypt after the battle of Pharsalus, with fatal results.

Other legislation that Caesar was keen to see ratified concerned the tightening up of the provincial administration. His *lex Julia de repetundis* dealing with extortion remained in force throughout most of the Empire. Such laws had long history throughout the Republic; they ensured that provincials could bring about a prosecution if they had been badly treated and recompense could be made. There was some reorganisation of the composition of the juries under the Gracchi and Sulla, and various additional clauses were added in successive laws. Caesar's was a synthesis of some of the clauses that had made up other laws as well as those dealing with cases of *repetundae*. He drew on a body of Roman and provincial experience, putting together a complex law that tried to take into account all possible scenarios. There were two aspects contained in the regulation of the behaviour of provincial governors; the protection of the inhabitants of the provinces was one aspect, and the other was the offence against the Roman state itself.

Caesar's relationship with Pompey was perhaps threatened by the suspect methods by which the legislation had been forced through. Pompey had declined to use such force when he experienced his problems with the Senate, even though he had seen his power and influence steadily eroded during the following years. He was involved too deeply with Caesar to back out, so he promised to meet swords with his own swords and shields, but he would undoubtedly have preferred to see the necessary measures to settle his veterans and to ratify his conquests all done by willing senatorial process. He was not entirely happy that his aims had to be achieved by an alliance with Caesar, and possibly even feared that he would be eclipsed by him, though in 59 the future Dictator was only partially visible in the consul and Pontifex Maximus. The two men would never entirely trust each other, but that does not mean that they would be eternally at loggerheads. Perhaps about April 59, their association was strengthened by marriage ties. Pompey had divorced his wife when he returned from the east, and his attempts to ally himself by marriage to the family of Cato had been spurned. So now he married Julia, Caesar's daughter. The consensus of contemporary and modern opinion is that this marriage was much more than a political expedient, and that Pompey fell head over heels for his new wife. The perhaps unexpected success of the marriage would proclaim even more loudly to a watching public that henceforth the First Man in Rome had thrown in his lot with Caesar. This left Crassus somewhat on a limb, cast in the role of the outsider, but not irrevocably divorced from the alliance.

In the summer of 59 the mysterious and probably insoluble case of Lucius Vettius flared up briefly and sputtered out. Vettius had been imprisoned by Caesar as praetor in 62. He already had a shaky reputation, and now he emerged with the alleged intention of fomenting a plot to murder Pompey. It was said that he had tried to involve Gaius Scribonius Curio, an avowed opponent of Caesar, in this plot, but the young man had refused to associate with him, and reported the matter to his father, one of Pompey's colleagues. At almost the same time, Bibulus got wind of a plot and warned Pompey against it. Vettius came before the Senate to answer for his actions, and started to name all sorts of eminent people who were supposedly implicated in the conspiracy. When Caesar brought him before the people's assembly next day the names that he gave out did not match those on his first list; it was notable that Marcus Brutus was no longer on it. Significantly, he was the son of Caesar's acknowledged mistress Servilia. People began to think that Vettius must somehow be a tool of Caesar's, and Cicero wrote to his friend Atticus along those lines. The motives and objectives of the main actors in this strange scenario remain worse than obscure. It may be that Vettius acted independently, having lost some of his sanity, and that he wanted to kill Pompey for motives of his own. It may be that others had concocted a plot to kill Pompey, and Vettius was made the scapegoat by persons unknown. Certain aristocrats may have used him in a bid to discredit Caesar by making it seem that he was behind it all. Caesar may in truth have been behind it all; some authors take it for granted that what he really wanted was to silence the young Curio who had spoken against him and sided with Cato and Bibulus. There is no evidence at all that can categorically lay the blame at anyone's door, but secrecy is after all the prime concern of plotters. Vettius had served in the army under Pompeius Strabo and was more likely Pompey's man than Caesar's, so it is possible that Pompey hatched a plot to discredit some of his opponents. Before it all became too embarrassing, Vettius somehow managed to strangle himself in prison; traditionally it was said that it was Vatinius who despatched him. And Vatinius was Caesar's man.

There remained the matter of a province for Caesar after his consulship ended. He intended from the first that it should be a long-term command involving military glory, and since Pompey had sorted out the eastern question for the time being, then Caesar had to look to the west or towards the Danube. There had already been warning signs of potential trouble in Gaul, where the chief of the Aedui, Diviciacus, appealed to Rome for help against the Sequani. The war threatened to escalate because in their struggle against the Aedui, the Sequani had called upon the German chief of the Suebi, Ariovistus, and he had gladly given assistance but demanded lands to settle some of his tribesmen within the territory of the Sequani. Everything appeared to be in turmoil: whole peoples were displaced; the Helvetii who had migrated to Switzerland from the Rhine and Main region now wanted to move again, and their route would probably take them through or near Roman territory. Rome had responded and prepared for war; recruitment had started, and Quintus Caecilius Metellus Celer and Lucius Afranius had drawn lots for the Gallic provinces. Metellus Celer was to be governor of Transalpine Gaul but unfortunately for him, and fortunately for Caesar, Celer died before he took up his command. Caesar obtained his proconsulship of Gaul in two stages, first Cisalpine Gaul and then Transalpine Gaul. By-passing the Senate, the tribune Vatinius proposed a new law in the people's assembly, that Caesar should become governor of Cisalpine Gaul and Illyricum, with three legions and a fixed term of five years. This was unequivocal; there was a specific terminal date before any other arrangements could be made for these provinces, specifically 1 March 54. The necessity for continuity of command and a reasonable term in which to achieve anything had been a lesson learned from previous experience; the tremendous power that could accrue from such a command had not been lost on Caesar. Unusually, Caesar was to receive the provinces with immediate effect, in the early summer of 59, which meant that he held a military command while still consul, with potential access to troops that would give him a slight edge in anything he proposed during the remainder of his office. At this stage it was not certain whether he would concentrate on Gaul, or whether he would perhaps be called upon to fight in Dacia, where the tribal leader Burebista was growing powerful. The command in Illyricum would allow him to turn rapidly towards Dacia with his troops. In 44 just before he was assassinated, Caesar still planned a Dacian campaign; he stationed troops in Macedonia in readiness to march to the Danube, intending to finish off the Danube problem and then march onwards to an eastern campaign. He never realised those ambitious plans in 44. After his first consulship in 59 he required a theatre of action that would still allow him to be close to Italy to monitor political events. Ultimately he chose Gaul as his theatre of action. With control of Cisalpine Gaul, he was well placed to observe what was happening in Rome and Italy, but a command in this province alone would not allow him to achieve very much in the military sphere. It was Pompey who proposed in the Senate that in addition to Cisalpine Gaul and Illyricum, Caesar should be given the province of Transalpine Gaul with one legion. This command was granted, and was to commence on 1 January 58 for one year, so it would have to be renewed annually.

Transalpine Gaul in its wider sense indicated the whole of Gaul beyond the Alps, but in the narrower sense of Roman territory it comprised the old province formed in 121 BC to protect the Greek colony and port of Massilia (modern Marseilles), and also the land route from Italy to Spain. The capital was at Narbo (modern Narbonne), which gave the province its later name of Gallia Narbonensis. In Caesar's day, the area under Roman control was referred to as the Province, *Provincia*, a name that still survives today as Provence. Beyond the Province, the Romans labelled the rest of the country Gallia Comata, which means Long-Haired Gaul. It was to be this area where Caesar would fight his battles, in lands that were outside his designated province.

When Caesar's consulship came to an end, the situation in Rome would change unless he could find some means of protecting his legislation and also some means of influencing political events. Caesar made a start on silencing or controlling potential opponents while he was still in office. In the spring of 59, Cicero took the opportunity at a trial to make a speech lamenting the current political situation. Having failed to win him over Caesar now laid the foundation for the political embarrassment and eventual exile of Cicero. On the same day that

9 Head of Caesar as an older man. Turin Museum; photo David Brearley

Cicero spoke out, Caesar as consul and Pontifex Maximus and Pompey as augur presided over a ceremony whereby the patrician Clodius transformed himself from a patrician into a plebeian, with the sole purpose of becoming tribune. He was adopted by the plebeian Publius Fonteius, a man younger than himself, simply to facilitate the procedure. Fonteius backed out of the arrangement once the formalities were over, and Clodius continued to call himself Clodius, and not, as he should have done, Fonteius Clodianus. He was elected tribune for 59/58. Though his life was already made miserable by Clodius, Cicero was granted some leeway before the new tribune took up office on the traditional date of 10 December 59. He started to agitate immediately, passing a law that outlawed anyone who had executed Roman citizens without a trial. Cicero knew precisely where Clodius' political and legal manoeuvrings were leading, and Caesar lingered near Rome for long enough to witness the gradual wearing down of the consul of 63 who had executed the five Catilinarians without trial. Caesar presumably felt some smug satisfaction when he was able to point out in a debate that he had warned of the consequences of such a peremptory act — a speech that could be summed up as 'I told you so and you didn't listen'. He reminded people that he had spoken against the death sentence at the time, but he also added that he did not approve of retrospective legislation such as Clodius had introduced. A lost cause, Cicero turned to Pompey for help, even going so far as to visit him at home, but Pompey exited at the back door as Cicero was shown in at the front. Voluntary exile was the only noble option before he faced trial, so Cicero packed and left. His house in Rome was pulled down.

Cato was the next to be removed. Clodius decided to annexe Cyprus, wresting it from the rule of the Ptolemies. It was said that Clodius held a grudge against Ptolemy Auletes because when he was held to ransom by pirates, and Ptolemy undertook to pay, he did not send enough cash. This cannot have been the only motive for annexation; trading and shipping interests will have entered the scene as well. The new province required a governor, and Cato was sent out to oversee the proceedings as Cyprus became a Roman acquisition. As Caesar entered his command in Gaul, two of the most persuasive speakers in Rome, who patently did not have his best interests at heart, had been removed. Clodius was active in other spheres. He introduced the free distribution of corn rations to the urban poor, always a politically motivated measure to pre-empt food riots and gain popularity. He also forbade the observation of the skies as a means of obstructing political business. At some point, he and Caesar had probably been to the same dinner party and talked earnestly for a while.

The rest of Clodius' tribuneship was nothing short of riotous. His street gangs controlled Rome and could be met only by more street gangs. Clodius had an agenda of his own that at best could be described as erratic and mercurial. If Caesar thought that he could use Clodius to control Rome in his absence then he had reckoned without the unscrupulousness and belligerent nature of his candidate. Clodius was no one's tool and performed only when it suited him. Perhaps Caesar's main aims were the removal of his opponents, and he did not much care about the mayhem he left behind. Like Pompey who sat back and waited to be asked to do something when there was a crisis, he may have thought that if things got too far out of hand he could return to Rome and quell the troubles, and then make the populace and the Senate grateful.

At some time during 59, Caesar married the daughter of Lucius Calpurnius Piso. Calpurnia remained his wife until his death, even though he had made tentative plans, which never came to fruition, to divorce her in order to marry the daughter of Pompey when their alliance was threatened. There is scant record of Calpurnia herself, but she was perhaps content to be married to the consul, who had by now emerged as a fully-fledged politician. There were indeed many Mariuses in him as Sulla had observed. He was clever, determined, ruthless, and as devious as the next man while maintaining an honest and noble facade, studiously moderate in all things, until he was thwarted, and then his actions revealed the diamond-hard core at the centre of this studied moderation. He was a staunch individualist, never content to be one among many. His ambition was plain for all to see, but it was not solely for his own personal gain. He was not interested in empty honours or political advancement for its own sake. He identified problems, and knew what was needed to solve them. He had broader vision than most, and thought in grandiose terms of the whole Roman world. He could see the best way of achieving the solutions to the problems he had identified, and was going to go directly for those solutions, sweeping aside anyone who did not share his version of the larger picture. He was going to do the best for Rome, whether Rome wanted it or not.

4 Gaul 58-52

Gaul was not a unified country with a central government and a capital city; the several tribal groups who inhabited what is now modern France would identify themselves first as Allobroges, or Aedui, or Senones, and only secondarily as Gauls. Inter-tribal rivalries engendered a restlessness that could be turned to advantage by any leader and band of followers who sought a cause for which to fight. Native chiefs allied with each other against other tribes or groups of tribes, and territorial boundaries could shift as a result; sometimes tribes could be absorbed by larger groups. Nascent states were emerging as Rome extended her influence into the Celtic west, but the concept of a city state like Rome, with a fixed territory and a corporate government that could make treaties, wage war and direct operations, had not yet universally taken root. The state was embodied in the king or chief; treaties and alliances were made on a personal basis, and were null and void when the leader died. The tribesmen related to eminent Romans in the same impermanent way, with the result that, when the representative that they knew and honoured was dead, they no longer considered themselves bound by the terms of any agreement they had made. There was much for Caesar to exploit in the activities and movements of the tribes in Gaul. His proconsulship had been deliberately chosen to bring him honour and glory to rival or even surpass Pompey, and provide him with enough wealth and influence to render him independent of anyone else in Rome for the rest of his career, however it was to unfold.

For some time the Helvetii, who had comparatively recently settled in what is now modern Switzerland, had felt themselves under pressure from their neighbours, the Germanic tribes across the Rhine, a perception that was heightened considerably when the Suebian Ariovistus arrived to help the Sequani. Potentially closed in and surrounded by Germanic tribes if the Suebi settled near to them, and especially if more of the transrhenine peoples began to follow, the Helvetii decided that avoidance was the best survival technique, and planned to move westwards to the territory of the Santones (modern Saintonge). Their route would take them through Geneva and the lands of the Allobroges; this route lay outside Roman territory, but it could be perceived as a threat to the Roman Province in southern Gaul. Caesar

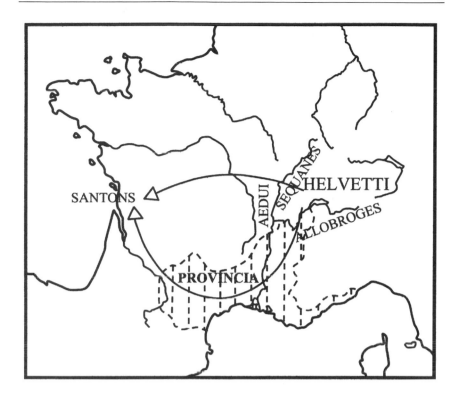

10 *The two possible migration routes of the Helvetii, one of which would have taken*
   them through the Roman Province, also known as Transalpine Gaul. It was in
   Caesar's interest to portray the migration as a definite danger to the Province, so
   that he would have an excuse to make war. Drawn by Jan Shearsmith after
   Fuller

had every intention of construing the movement of the Helvetii as a
potentially hostile act, in order to create a war for himself. The Helvetii
had once defeated Roman armies, and had a reputation as a fierce and
warlike enemy. Fear and loathing, and a desire for revenge, coupled with
a desire for the glory that such revenge would carry in its wake, all
contributed to Caesar's rapid decision to act.

Having lingered near Rome long enough to see Cicero despatched
into exile, Caesar dashed northwards in March 58 to organise defence
from Geneva. The Helvetii had built a bridge across the Rhône. Caesar
destroyed it and then erected a fortified barrier along the river valley to
prevent the passage of the tribes. The effect was to turn the Helvetii to a
different and more difficult route, this time through the territory of the
Sequani. Caesar declared that this was just as much a threat to Roman
territory, but with the three legions voted to him in Vatinius' law he could

not stop the migration once it had begun, so he hurried back to Cisalpine Gaul to recruit two more legions, leaving Titus Labienus in command on the Rhône. Strictly, the men whom he enrolled ought to have been Roman citizens, a distinction that the Cisalpine Gauls did not yet possess, but Caesar was never one for rules and regulations when speed and expediency were required. Besides, his recruitment drive held out the tacit promise that Roman citizenship was within the bounds of possibility for the Gauls on the Italian side of the Alps.

The Helvetii passed through the lands of the Aedui and Allobroges, causing damage, probably aggressively foraging for food, perhaps even pillaging. The afflicted tribes appealed to Caesar for protection, which gave him a cast iron excuse for conducting a war that he had every intention of conducting anyway. In his account of the Gallic wars, written in 51, Caesar is careful to set out the reasons for this war and the necessities of waging it.

His allies were not united in their support. The Aedui were split into two opposing groups, one led by Diviciacus, who appealed to Caesar, and the other led by Dumnorix, the brother of Diviciacus, who had set his hopes on an agreement with the Helvetii. Caesar followed the Helvetii to the river Saone, where he held a meeting with their leaders, but this concourse came to nothing and the whole tribe pressed on. Difficulties beset the Roman pursuit. When the Aeduan horsemen attached to the army were attacked, they scattered and fled. The food supplies were deliberately disrupted; the culprit was Dumnorix. Caesar placed him under guard. In order to secure supplies, Caesar diverted his march and aimed for Bibracte (Mount Beuvray), the capital of the Aedui, but the Helvetii construed the manoeuvre as a retreat, so they followed and attacked. In the ensuing battle, the whole tribe was present, with the women and children and the baggage drawn up behind the warriors, potentially blocking their route if they needed to withdraw. Caesar was probably outnumbered, and as the battle progressed he also had to deal with a flank attack by the Celtic Boii and Tulingi, which nearly stopped the Roman advance, especially when the Helvetii took advantage of the panic and surged forwards again. The fighting lasted until nightfall, and in the end the Helvetii were broken and repulsed. Survivors fled towards the territory of the Lingones. Caesar let it be known that if assistance were offered to the scattered tribesmen, such acts would warrant a declaration of war. Ultimately the remnants of the Helvetii were sent back to their homes, which they themselves had destroyed when their migration began. They rebuilt them, and took on the task imposed on them of keeping the Germanic tribes beyond them at bay.

Caesar had fought and won his first battle. There was no training school for generals in Rome, and even after the reforms of Marius there was no long-established, permanent professional army with an officer cadre who could pass on experience and expertise. There had been only a little time to learn about such matters at Marius' knee, but somehow Caesar had learned how to command an army with an almost casual daring and a veritable flare. Within months of assembling an army Caesar had welded his troops together, inspired them with confidence in themselves and in him, and led them to victory over an enemy who had once forced captured Romans to pass under the yoke as a token of submission. The report that Caesar sent to Rome would not be a modest little note.

The next stage of Caesar's Gallic war centred on Ariovistus and the Suebi, brought into Gaul by the Sequani in their feud with the Aedui. The theme for the Romans was once again the protection of their Aeduan allies, threatened now by the further influx of Suebi following in the footsteps of the more select band who had settled in Gaul. The Sequani who had started it all were powerless to stop them, nor were the Aedui any better placed to protect their territory. For the Romans there was one problem in declaring war upon Ariovistus and his warriors, in that Caesar himself had been instrumental in proclaiming him a friend and ally of the Roman people only the year before. Diplomatic wrangling preceded the fighting, so that Caesar could be seen to have pursued all possible channels to find a peaceful solution to the problem. He asked politely if Ariovistus could restrict his followers to the agreed boundaries. This would mean that the Suebi would have to abandon territory that Ariovistus regarded as his by right of conquest. Naturally he refused. Stage one on the road to war had been passed. Caesar would have been quite irritated if Ariovistus had meekly withdrawn, because then another excuse would have to be found for fighting him. Stage two involved demands from Caesar. First he underlined the fact that the Aedui were under Roman protection, and war would be inevitable if they were disturbed or threatened in any way. Secondly, Caesar absolutely forbade any further movements of the Suebi across the Rhine. If these conditions were not met then the friendship of the Roman people would be withdrawn from Ariovistus.

Preparing for confrontation, Caesar moved to the capital of the Sequani at Vesontio (modern Besançon) to prevent Ariovistus from occupying it. At this point the Roman troops began to lose heart, because the reputation of the Germanic tribes such as the Suebi was fearsome. It was time to make a stirring speech and a grand gesture, something for which Caesar was particularly talented and for which he would be renowned. He reminded the soldiers that the Cimbri and Teutones had been defeated, perhaps implying that he had absorbed some special techniques in fighting tribesmen from his kinsman Marius. Finally he

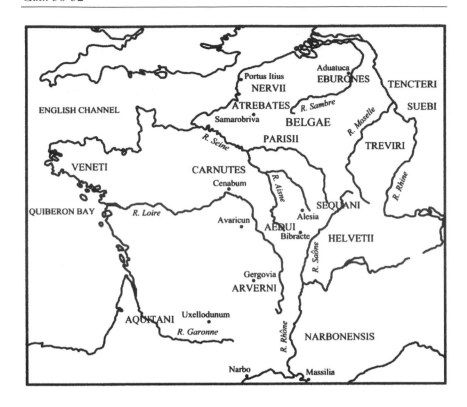

11 *Map of Gaul showing the principal tribes. Caesar interpreted his governorship of Transalpine Gaul very loosely, and most of his term of office was spent in territory that was strictly outside his allocated province.* Drawn by Jan Shearsmith

said that if the troops were afraid then he would face the enemy alone with the Tenth legion which he trusted with his life. The soldiers had known him long enough now to have formed their opinion of their commander; they probably believed that he would do exactly what he said. And after his speech the Tenth legion would have followed him into Hades if he had he asked them to do so. Whatever he said and however he said it, the magic worked. Six days later the Roman army was drawn up within about a day's march of Ariovistus' camp. According to Caesar's own account there was a meeting of the two leaders, in the course of which each of them outlined their relative positions. The speeches as reported by Caesar may embody the content of the discourse, but of course they serve as a useful and dramatic exposition of the plot, each opposing viewpoint neatly condensed for the Roman audiences who would hear or read the account of the Gallic war. Caesar's main point was that although most of Gaul was technically free, Rome's interests in the whole country were paramount, therefore infiltration or conquest by another power could not be condoned. In a nutshell what Caesar really meant was that if anyone was going to conquer Gaul it would be him, not a Germanic chief from across the Rhine. There was no further parley. Ariovistus proposed another meeting but Caesar declined the offer. Ariovistus responded by seizing Caesar's envoys sent to give notice of his refusal to meet again. Then he marched his tribesmen off and took up a position to the rear of Caesar's camp, threatening the Roman supply lines and communications. To protect these lines Caesar built a smaller camp a short distance from the first.

He offered battle fruitlessly for five days. There was a skirmish outside the smaller Roman camp on the sixth day, then on the seventh day the real battle commenced, progressing so rapidly that the two sides closed before the Romans had chance to throw their spears. Instead they drew their swords and went straight in. Caesar had calculated that Ariovistus' left wing was his weakest point so he stationed himself on his own right wing to direct operations. On his left wing he owed his eventual success to the prompt action of Publius Licinius Crassus, the son of Marcus Crassus. This officer brought troops up in support when the wing began to falter; Caesar made special mention of it in his account of the wars. The end result of the battle was the complete dispersal of Ariovistus' forces and, arising from Caesar's success, the Suebi who were about to cross the Rhine decided against entering into Gaul and turned back.

It had been a highly satisfactory first campaign. Caesar called a halt, placing the troops in winter quarters under the command of Titus Labienus, while he himself went to Cisalpine Gaul where the civil government of the province claimed his attention. From his headquarters he could communicate with his agents in Rome more easily, though he was never entirely out of touch with political developments there. For the time being Clodius was ruling the roost in Rome. Mercurial, irresponsible and far too self-centred to act as a willing agent for anyone, Clodius had turned against Pompey with a vengeance, going so far as to hatch a plot to assassinate him, and when it came to nothing he used his henchmen to besiege the great man in his own house. This does not mean that Clodius was a confirmed partisan of Pompey's enemies, or of any party at all. His next move was to try to have all Caesar's acts of his consulship declared illegal because they had all been put into effect when Bibulus was watching the heavens for omens, and all public business ought to have been cancelled. Clodius' actions ultimately benefited neither him nor anyone else, and Caesar probably did not lose any sleep over the young man's shenanigans. On another matter he was more reserved. Agitation had started for the recall of Cicero. One of the tribunes who proposed it went to meet Caesar to sound him out, but

Caesar did not receive the idea with unrestrained joy. The proposal was dropped, and would remain in abeyance until Pompey and his lieutenants managed to set up a rival gang to counter the continual violence or threat of violence from Clodius. Caesar has been accused of using Clodius to disrupt political life, but modern authors have doubted it. Clodius was a law unto himself, acting independently for purposes which are rarely if ever crystal clear, and inconsistently when it suited him to change his tactics.

The presence of the Romans in Gaul made the tribes of the interior nervous and restless. They no doubt knew that his command of the Cisalpine province was to last for four more years, and by now it was clear that he had no intention of spending those years peacefully administering the law and founding colonies. The Celtic and Germanic tribes recognised a fire-eating general when they encountered one. Consequently some of the tribes began to make common cause and to arm in readiness for the war that they felt sure would eventually come. Labienus had agents with receptive antennae, who gathered information that the various groups of the Belgae of north-western Gaul had formed a coalition. Caesar began to move in early spring with two new legions, the Thirteenth and Fourteenth, that he had raised in Cisalpine Gaul. Diviciacus and his Aeduan cavalry and infantry were also at Caesar's disposal, so he sent them to harass the Bellovaci to prevent them from joining the main group of the Belgae. Caesar made for the territory of the Remi, around modern Rheims and Châlons. The Remi submitted instantly, throwing in their lot with the Romans and handing over the hostages that Caesar demanded. In return the Romans beat off a Belgic attack on one of the settlements of the Remi.

Operations shifted to the river Aisne. Somewhere along its course Caesar fortified a bridge and crossed to the northern bank where he built a camp. The Belgae soon followed, selecting a site to the north of the Roman troops, where they made their own camp. They tried to circle round and come up behind Caesar by crossing the river some distance away and doubling back, but Caesar defeated them with a cavalry attack. The Romans had attended to logistics and had secured their supply lines, so it was now a question of waiting until the tribesmen ran out of food and were forced to move. When they did so, Caesar was not sure at first whether this was just a ruse to draw him on in pursuit. Then he moved himself, sending the cavalry to dog the heels of the tribesmen while he advanced on and occupied the native towns of the Suessiones and Bellovaci to suppress any warlike activity.

He moved on to the river Sambre. There he faced the Nervii, the Viromandui and the Atrebates, contingents of the federation of the Belgae. He was badly prepared for this encounter. While the army was still on the march and the legionaries of the vanguard were setting up camp near the river, the tribesmen chose their moment well and attacked. There was only a cavalry screen protecting the builders of the camp instead of the forces that Caesar normally posted to serve this function, and the horsemen were quickly dispersed. The tribesmen burst across the river and took the Romans by surprise. Fortunately the legionaries were disciplined enough not to waste time trying to form up with their proper units, and simply gathered round the nearest standard. They had fought two campaigns during the previous summer against two different native adversaries, so they held firm against the onslaught. On Caesar's right, the Nervii began to push the Romans back and threatened to come round behind them, so despite the fact that the Viromandui and the Atrebates were forced back across the river it seemed that the Nervii might win the day. Caesar was now fighting not only for his reputation but also his life. He rose to the challenge with panache, rushing to the scene, borrowing a shield and somehow pushing his way to the front, calling to the centurions by name, then sounding the charge. His career might have ended on this gloriously brave note had it not been for the simultaneous arrival of the two recently recruited legions who were last in the line of march, and of the Tenth legion under Labienus who managed to disengage from the battle on the other side of the river and then sandwich the Nervii between that legion and the two less experienced ones. The Nervii were obliterated. The remaining tribesmen came to terms, which were lenient enough. The tribesmen were to keep their lands, and other tribes were warned not to attack them. Caesar was merciful. He could afford to be. The only Nervii left were the few survivors of the battle, the women, children and old men. These remnants, however, were to give a good account of themselves in the winter of 54.

Command of an army seemed to come naturally to Caesar. The fact that he knew the names of the centurions in the front line of the battle cannot be overestimated as an attribute of a general. Attention to that sort of detail engenders not only affection and loyalty in the troops, but also total confidence. His physical presence in the thick of the fighting was the equivalent of at least another legion; as Wellington said of Napoleon, on the battlefield his hat was worth 50,000 men. Caesar was well served by his subordinates, and he struck the balance between too tight a rein that stifled independent thought or action, and the loose control that permitted far too much licence. He had identified Titus Labienus and Publius Crassus as trustworthy officers who could act on their own initiative, and his investment paid off. But ultimately both these subordinates and all the soldiers knew who was really in control.

Caesar's report to the Senate was well received, and even his enemies had to admit that it was a momentous achievement to extend Roman arms into uncharted territory. Trading interests would soon follow where the army led. The Romans did not think in terms of humanitarian questions, so the near annihilation of the Nervii would be just an unfortunate consequence of Rome's inexorable advance. The climate in Rome had changed subtly. Pompey had managed to curb the wilder activities of Clodius by resorting to the same violent tactics. His gangs were marshalled by Titus Annius Milo; but of course on the face of it Pompey's hands were clean, and people were glad to see that someone could subdue Clodius a little. Another change on the political scene was the return of Cicero in the summer of 57. After failing the first time round, Pompey grew more determined and brought about the orator's recall. Both Cicero and Pompey spoke in favour of Caesar in the Senate, voting him an extraordinary 15 days of thanksgiving for his victories. Pompey had merited only ten days for his eastern campaigns.

Caesar spent the autumn in Illyricum, which he had hitherto neglected. His main focus of attention was, as always, concentrated on Rome. Despite the honours voted to him after the campaigns of the summer, he was less secure now than he had been at the beginning of his command. Technically he had only two more seasons in which to conclude his business in Gaul, and it was nowhere near finished to his satisfaction. And Pompey was building up another power base by means of an extraordinary command to regulate the corn supply, with powers for five years and a staff of 15 legates to assist him. The strain on the food supply of Rome was increased by Clodius' institution of the corn dole to the urban poor, and there had been riots in the city. Who but Pompey could be entrusted with such a task, and one that would bring such acclaim? Pompey might soon eclipse Caesar, because he was dealing with matters of immediate interest, while Caesar was far away and dealing with problems that did not affect the populace at first hand. The partnership of three that had launched Caesar on his consulship and proconsulship was fragmenting. Each of the partners was intent on pursuing his own career, without reference to the needs of the other two. Despite his glorious conquests it was Caesar who was out on a limb, because he had no physical presence at the hub of political life. He had considerable influence through his agents, one of whom was the wealthy Cornelius Balbus, and he could ensure that some members of his circle were elected to appropriate magistracies, but because of the distances involved he was unable to react swiftly to the rapid shifts in political life, staying one step ahead. If Pompey and Crassus were striking out independently it would reduce the number of magistrates that Caesar could hope to control by himself. As his influence weakened there would be opportunities for his enemies to introduce harmful legislation aimed at bringing down the edifice he had built up during his consulship. Already at the end of 57 the tribune Publius Rutilius Rufus had set about dismantling Caesar's agrarian law, and Lucius Domitius Ahenobarbus was intent on removing him from his Gallic command. If that came about, Caesar would not be able to step into another office and would be a private citizen, prey to all kinds of litigation. His chosen candidates as tribunes and other magistrates were not always successful in carrying out his wishes. He needed more political weight.

As part of his inspection of the provinces under his command he came to Ravenna in the spring of 56, and met up with Crassus. Who had contacted whom is not known, but the meeting will have been arranged some time before, as was the next meeting at Luca in April, where Pompey was also present. The three of them confidently carved up the Roman world and undertook to direct the course of Roman politics for the next decade or so. Pompey and Crassus were to be consuls for 55; bribery, corruption and the presence of lots of Caesar's soldiers in Rome at the time of the elections made this proposal a certainty. They were also to receive proconsular commands equal to Caesar's, and Caesar's command was to be confirmed and extended. Following the example of the *lex Vatinia*, they were all to insulate themselves against senatorial influence for five years by setting a definite terminal date for their commands, before which no discussion was to be permitted. The date that was eventually set for discussion of Pompey's command and that of Crassus was 1 March 50, but it is not known if the same arrangement was definitely made for Caesar's proconsulship of Gaul. The lack of certainty as to the legal termination of his command makes it impossible to unravel the exact political position that Caesar occupied in 50 and 49, but the salient factor is that he hoped to retain his army and his command while he stood for the consulship, and hopefully glide seamlessly and unassailably from military command to consul designate, then to consul, without an interval as a private citizen who would be susceptible to prosecutions under various headings that his enemies were probably already drafting clause by clause. A great deal of modern ink has flowed in the cause of elucidating the finer details of this arrangement, but the most important point is that the three men felt themselves powerful enough to bring Roman political life under their control and to remain in control for the foreseeable future. Naturally their ambitious plans were not widely broadcast, though the news could scarcely be kept secret that both Crassus and Pompey had travelled northwards, when Pompey at least ought to have been going in the opposite direction to attend to the corn supply.

From Caesar's point of view, he had brought in the most powerful agents to ensure that he extended his command of Cisalpine and

Illyricum beyond the five years originally conferred on him by Vatinius' law, and his command of Transalpine Gaul, granted him through the agency of Pompey, would be confirmed and assured. This command was where his future glory was to be found. He would never have been contented solely with the Cisalpine province, and the rugged terrain of Illyricum precluded swift, sweeping victories. With the assurance that Pompey and Crassus would attend to his needs, he had given himself a breathing space and deferred any discussion about when he should be recalled until a future date. He could now achieve so much more in the time allowed him, and his plans were ambitious, including an invasion of Britain. It may be that this proposal had leaked out, and caused consternation among the coastal tribes in the north west of Gaul. They formed a coalition, perhaps because they anticipated that any invasion of Britain would involve the subjugation of the tribes and the control of their territory. Publius Crassus had been sent to arrange the submission of the Veneti and other tribes in the area now occupied by Normandy and Brittany, and at first they had all readily agreed on friendship with the Romans. But their resistance stiffened during the winter, and when Crassus sent envoys to negotiate the supplies of corn for the army, the Veneti detained them, demanding the return of their hostages. Such recalcitrance provided Caesar with all the just cause that he needed to make war. Since this would be fought at sea as well as on land, he ordered the building of warships on the Loire. He gave the command of the fleet to Decimus Brutus, while he himself attended to the land battles.

The fleet could make little progress against an experienced enemy like the Veneti, who were expert seamen, familiar with the ports and inlets and the vagaries of the tides and the weather. Their strongly built ships were well adapted to the rough seas that were frequent on the coast, and also the low tides, where they were in less danger than the Roman ships of going aground. Decimus Brutus achieved nothing until he developed the technique of bringing down their yardarms and sails by means of grappling hooks on long poles. After being mauled in this way, the Veneti tried to escape by sailing further out to sea, but they were suddenly becalmed, and waited like sitting ducks to be attacked and disabled one by one.

Caesar was able to secure the whole area and the coast. He turned the imprisonment of Crassus' envoys into an international incident and used it as the excuse to eliminate the leading men of the Veneti. The rest he sold into slavery. It remained to mop up resistance from smaller coastal tribes nearer to the Rhine. Caesar conducted a very long march to flush them out, but succeeded only in forcing the tribes into hiding in the forests. He did not waste time trying to bring them to battle; a winter campaign in forested country would be foolhardy and profitless. He could begin again next spring. It was inevitable that he would have to pick up the threads where he left off. The movements of the Suebi had displaced other tribes on the Rhine, among them the Usipetes and Tencteri, who crossed the river in the winter in search of new lands. The danger was that they would ally with the Gallic tribes who were disaffected, particularly the Belgae in north-western Gaul. As Caesar approached the scene of action, the Tencteri and the Usipetes sent representatives to him to explain that circumstances had forced them to leave their homes, and that they wanted to settle in Gaul. Cautious and distrustful, Caesar negotiated with the Ubii who lived close to the Rhine and who had submitted to him, to allow the new arrivals to settle in their territory. A series of delaying tactics ensued for the next few days while the tribesmen stalled for time under the heading of negotiations and Caesar pressed on closer and closer, professing to agree to their terms not to advance beyond certain points. He camped a short distance from the tribesmen, promising to receive their envoys next day. Until this meeting was over there was supposed to be a truce, but some German cavalry attacked Caesar's Gallic cavalry, thus providing an immediate excuse for Caesar's next action, treacherous, but coldly expedient. The tribal leaders came to his camp as arranged, to parley. He took them all prisoner and then mounted a surprise attack on the Germans in their camp. It was a massacre, continuing all the way to the Rhine as the Romans chased the tribesmen and the women and children. Those who were not killed by the army were finished off in the waters of the Rhine.

The point had been made that Caesar would not tolerate the infiltration of German tribes into Gaul, but he followed it up with a celebrated demonstration of strength and Roman ingenuity by building a bridge to carry his army across the Rhine. The plentiful forests provided the timber, and the army completed the task in ten days. His description of the bridge and how it was built does not clarify all the details, with the result that more than one reconstruction is possible by several different methods. Caesar's bridge was the subject of a recent TV programme, where engineers using the instructions that can be derived from the passage in the *Gallic War* attempted to build the first few piers of the bridge. The problems that they encountered only serve to emphasise the expertise of the Roman army. The Romans crossed into German territory and the tribes prepared for war, but Caesar was interested only in making a display of Roman prowess and not in fighting. He returned to Gaul after only a few days, and destroyed the bridge to prevent the Germans from using it. He left them in no doubt that he could build any number of bridges if he felt the need, and penetrate right to the heart of the tribal territory. His demonstration was a mixture of conviction, ability, bluster and bluff, and fortunately the Germans never called his bluff.

After crossing the Rhine Caesar set his sights on crossing something rather more imposing, the narrow sea that separated Britain from the European mainland. The projected invasion of Britain, which had probably contributed to the unrest among the Veneti, would have to be either abandoned for this year or curtailed because winter was approaching. There would be time for a quick reconnaissance of the southern parts of the country, nothing more. It was not an entirely unknown land, since there had been considerable contact between Britain and Gaul, and there was a flourishing cross-Channel trade in which Roman goods already featured. It may even have been true, as Caesar alleged, that the Britons had sent help to the Gauls and provided refuge for them when they fled. This was the official reason for the landing in Britain, but the desire for fame to match Pompey's will have played some part as well, as will the need to go on and on, to prolong the need for a military command.

As a preliminary he sent Gaius Volusenus, an officer in whom he had great faith, to reconnoitre the coast to find suitable landing places in Britain. Modern historians have criticised Caesar for not using the port of Richborough, which was well known to the Romans who did occupy the island in the first century AD, but, as Salway points out in his history of Roman Britain, since there was a hundred-year gap between Caesar's invasion and that of Claudius, the choice of Richborough may not have seemed so excellent to Volusenus. In order to sound out the tribes, Caesar despatched to Britain the man whom he had installed as the king of the Gallic Atrebates, Commius. His task was to spread the word that the Romans were coming, and to encourage as many people as he could to submit to Caesar.

The fleet that Caesar assembled was small, comprising the galleys that he had built for the war against the Veneti, and some ships from the coastal tribes of Gaul that he had commandeered. Leaving from two separate ports, almost certainly Boulogne, and perhaps also from Ambleteuse, Caesar took the Seventh and Tenth legions and some cavalry, but the horse transports were unable to land in the stormy weather, so it was with infantry alone that Caesar faced the British opposition. The cliffs were lined with tribesmen, who marched overland, following the Roman ships as they sailed round the coast, probably to Deal where the battle began. The troops were reluctant to disembark, but the standard bearer of the Tenth legion leapt into the shallow water and headed for the shore with the standard held high, so all could see that it would be captured unless the soldiers followed. According to Caesar's account, the Britons still used chariots in battle, a fighting method that had gone out of fashion on the continent. Caesar admired the nimble handling of the chariots, which were manned by a charioteer and a warrior. Once the battle was fully engaged, the charioteer deposited the warrior who fought on foot while the chariots withdrew to await the outcome. In the event of a defeat, the tribesmen could escape via this Iron Age equivalent of a rapid transit system.

Despite their skills and their bravery the Britons were defeated and submitted to Caesar, delivering the hostages that were demanded of them, but they quickly rallied when the unpredictable weather caused considerable embarrassment to the Romans. The cavalry in the horse transports were once again prevented from landing, and worse still the gales drove Caesar's ships onto the shore. He had neglected to beach them properly to keep them out of the way of the rough tides, and as a result he lost twelve ships. The rest were damaged but not irretrievably so. The loss of his transports back to Gaul could have been disastrous, especially as the Britons seized the moment to launch an attack on the Seventh legion while the soldiers were out foraging. Caesar rallied the troops and led them to victory, but it had been a close call. He ought to have been prepared for the storms, and should have anticipated an attack while he repaired his ships, but since he surmounted these difficulties he had no problem in telling it more or less as it was in his brief account of his exploits. When the weather calmed down, he withdrew and sailed back to Gaul. Two of the British tribes sent hostages, but none of the rest did so. Apart from vast personal kudos and some slight knowledge of Britain, Caesar had accomplished much but ultimately gained very little.

Although his successes from 58 to 55 had been lauded and celebrated in Rome, a voice of dissent was heard in the Senate. Cato was back. He had been thwarted of the praetorship by the intrigues and lavish bribery of Pompey and Crassus, the consuls for 55. He objected to Caesar's treatment of the German tribes who had been thrown back across the Rhine, and made speeches damaging to Caesar and his reputation. Cato's concern with the fate of the Germans was merely a stick with which to beat Caesar, nothing to do with sympathy for northern tribes who were being steadily forced off their lands. In a different context, if it suited his purpose, he would have been just as ardent in his recommendation that the Germans should be annihilated, man, woman and child. But it is incontrovertible that Caesar had waged war more or less for his own ends, and had repeatedly seized upon the slenderest of excuses to embark on wars. In this he was not alone, in fact it was a pronounced Roman trait, but it was all grist to Cato's mill, especially when Caesar replied to his attacks by means of a letter which his friends read out in the Senate. Silence would have been more appropriate, because Cato was roused to further eloquence, and if Caesar had won the military wars in Gaul, then Cato had won the verbal wars in Rome.

While Caesar had been engaged against the German tribes Pompey and Crassus had been organising Roman politics and consolidating their position. They gained the consulship for 55, not without dire opposition, and they filled as many magistracies as possible with their own and Caesar's adherents. The tribune Gaius Trebonius proposed the bill allocating the provinces of Spain and Syria for five years to the outgoing consuls when they stepped down in 54. There was to be no discussion of replacement or recall until 1 March 50. The bill did not have an easy passage into law; Cato tried his best to defeat it, and in the rioting that ensued there were deaths. Before the year ended, Crassus departed for Syria, intent on a campaign against the Parthians. Pompey merely sent his legates to Spain, and never left Rome.

More important for Caesar, the two consuls honoured their arrangement to extend and confirm his command, perhaps like their own, to the agreed date of 1 March 50. The problems about the date have already been mentioned (above p71). Secure in his appointment, or as secure as he could hope to be, Caesar planned a second expedition to Britain. He had given orders to his officers to build more ships and to repair the old ones, and at the beginning of the year he had 600 transports and 28 galleys. Before he could embark the troops he had to suppress a hostile coalition of several of the Gallic chieftains, instigated and led by Dumnorix. The Treveri had gone further and made overtures to the Germans, but fortunately for Caesar the Treveri were disunited, with two rival leaders who both claimed supremacy. All Caesar had to do was to promote one at the expense of the other, so when Cingetorix voluntarily submitted to him, he bestowed on him full Roman support, rejecting the claims of Indutiomarus, who submitted involuntarily and surrendered hostages. Once this was settled, Caesar journeyed to Portus Itius (Boulogne) to embark his legions, summoning the Gallic chiefs to meet him there. They arrived, not suspecting that Caesar was about to take them all hostage and carry them to Britain with him. Dumnorix refused to let himself be captured so easily, and fled, but he was overtaken and killed.

The second British invasion started in July, with a huge fleet of 800 ships, according to Caesar's account. The Britons were overawed and did not even attempt to oppose the landing. Instead they took up a position on high ground and waited for the Romans to come to them. Caesar left his ships at anchor in order to disembark the troops and get them marching more quickly. It would have wasted valuable time to beach them, and he would have lost the momentum in engaging in battle. But there were probably a few backward glances and not a little grumbling among the soldiers who knew all about the damage to the ships caused by the storm in the previous year. Perhaps Caesar thought along the lines of the old adage that lightning does not strike twice; but unfortunately, this time it did. The storm this time wrecked more ships because while they were riding at anchor they collided with each other. Caesar was forced to return to the coast, where he placed Labienus in charge of repairing the ships.

The Britons made common cause and settled their differences under the leadership of the chief of the Catuvellauni, a man called Cassivellaunus, who knew that open battle was the last thing he should attempt and that guerrilla tactics would be more effective. Nonetheless, he did make a stand. Caesar marched cautiously inland, until he met the Britons at the Thames, where they had fortified the riverbank with stakes. The Romans in Caesar's army had some years' battle experience by now, and did not let the river itself or the fortifications stop their advance. It was a victory, offset by the fact that Cassivellaunus roused the Kentish tribes to attack the troops who were repairing the ships at the naval base.

As he progressed further inland, Caesar needed to cultivate allies among the tribes who could lend him support, and deny it to Cassivellaunus. He made great play of generous treatment of the Trinobantes whose crops he spared, and they submitted to him. Shortly afterwards Cassivellaunus followed suit and asked for terms. The Britons were not uneducated savages. They were aware of what was happening in Gaul and in Rome, and Cassivellaunus and his associates had probably arrived at the conclusion that Caesar was not intent on complete conquest of Britain, and that he would have enough to do in Gaul to consolidate the Roman conquest and make all the arrangements for the administration of the country. He probably also knew that Caesar's main aims in all this warmongering were focused on Rome, and the achievement of the supreme position there would necessarily take him away from the provinces and from Britain. For Cassivellaunus, surrender was more likely a short-term means of bringing the war to a conclusion, rather than a humiliating long-term defeat. Caesar exacted immediate tribute, which the Britons perhaps readily assembled and paid in order to see the back of the Roman army and the fleet so much more speedily. The Britons were not to see another invading Roman army for the best part of a century.

The two expeditions to Britain brought no profit to Rome and nothing but a reputation for daring to Caesar. If there had been rumours of vast wealth to be gained, then they had proved false. But the exploit left an enduring example, one that Claudius emulated, but with the purpose of annexation and pacification, which Caesar cannot have

12 *Head of Mark*
   Antony, as he may
   have appeared
   when he first
   joined Caesar in
   Gaul. Courtesy
   Capitoline
   Museum, Rome

contemplated. He left no troops behind to hold onto his gains and did not actively pursue the payment of tribute and the surrender of hostages. He would have weakened his army if he had tried to garrison even a small part of Britain, and he was not ready to reduce his armed support; he might need it one day to stay in power.

Alliances in Rome shifted slightly in 54. Cicero was always ambivalent about Caesar, wanting to like him, but disliking his politics. He recognised the fact that Caesar could not be ignored and ultimately would have to be faced either as a friend or an enemy. As a friend he could perhaps be used. Cicero obtained an appointment for his brother Quintus on Caesar's staff, and he borrowed money from him. It was not a match made in Heaven, but the two could be of mutual benefit to each other. Caesar could use Cicero as an agent in Rome to do him small favours, and Cicero advanced his brother's career and restarted his own. They corresponded amicably enough. If Caesar had been a more mediocre general and politician, he and Cicero might have been good friends.

A more deeply personal event of 54 was the death of Caesar's daughter Julia. She died trying to give birth to Pompey's son. The child died shortly after. It may be significant that Cornelius Balbus, who was with Caesar in Britain, was sent to Rome as soon as the expeditionary army returned to Gaul, possibly to sound out Pompey and shore up the alliance. Opinion is divided about the influence of Julia over Pompey and Caesar and how different the subsequent history of Rome might have been if she had lived longer. The speculators of a more reasonable nature argue that Julia could have contributed much to the continuation of the alliance between her husband and father, while the more hard-headed insist that personal ambition and the course of politics would have divided Pompey from Caesar sooner or later. If Caesar grieved it was in stalwart Roman tradition, inwardly, while fulfilling his duties as governor. It probably gratified him to learn that Julia's funeral had been taken over by the people of Rome, who decided that she should be laid to rest in the Campus Martius, and carried her body there by force. It was an honour for Caesar, and he acknowledged it as such.

During the winter of 54/3 Caesar remained in Transalpine Gaul. The weather had been inclement and unkind to crops, and the harvests had been dismal. The legions could not be quartered close to each other since they would eat each other out of house and home, or perhaps tent and fort, so each one had to camp some distance from the others so that their foraging areas would not overlap. Before all the arrangements were finalised, the occupants of one of the camps were annihilated. The Treveran chief Indutiomarus was still resentful that his claim for supremacy had been squashed by Caesar, and he had since devoted himself to spreading disaffection against the Romans among other tribes. He encouraged Ambiorix, chief of the Eburones, to attack the Romans encamped at Aduatuca, which he did in a rather half-hearted fashion. A siege would have been out of the question, so Ambiorix resorted to subterfuge. He sent a message to the commanders Sabinus and Cotta that he had attacked only because he was obliged to do so, as part of a plot that had spread among the Gauls to launch an assault on all the Roman camps at once. He convinced the Romans that the German tribes were also involved and that some tribesmen were en route for their camp at that very moment. He pointed out that there was strength in numbers, and that it would be better to leave their fortified camp and march to join Quintus Cicero, whose camp was about two day's journey from theirs, in the vicinity of Namur. Cotta and the officers were against making any move, but Sabinus and the soldiers overruled them. The troops marched out and were slaughtered. Only a few escaped and reached Labienus' camp, where they passed on the gory details.

This success encouraged other tribes to take to arms. The Nervii put Quintus Cicero's camp under siege, adapting their techniques to Roman methods; being soundly defeated is after all an educative process. Cicero erected more fortifications and towers, defending his camp ably, but he was aware that as the siege went on his soldiers would be less and less able to withstand attacks. Caesar was at Amiens, where Cicero tried to send messages. After a few failed attempts, one messenger did get through, and Caesar acted with characteristic speed. He summoned troops from other camps but by this time Labienus was pinned down by Indutiomarus, so it was with fewer troops than he would have preferred that Caesar approached Cicero's camp. The Nervii broke off the siege to meet him. According to Caesar's account he was outnumbered by about ten to one, so a pitched battle was out of the question. He chose his own scene of action, positively inviting the Nervii to attack his camp, which he built on an extremely small scale as though he had even fewer troops than he had in reality. He ordered the legionaries to simulate disorder and panic. The Nervii read all the signals and concluded that an attack would be a walkover, but once they had launched themselves on the camp, Caesar's men rushed out from all the gates and attacked from all directions. The cavalry dispersed the rest of the tribesmen.

The forests soon swallowed up the Nervii, so Caesar wasted no time on pursuing and flushing them out, instead marching straight to Cicero's camp. When Indutiomarus heard of the failure of the Nervii he raised the siege of Labienus' camp. His influence on the Gauls had been pronounced, but without him there was a lull in Gallic ardour. Then the Treveri and the Eburones allied and other tribes started to arm, and there was the perennial threat posed by the Germans who might at any moment cross the Rhine. Caesar took these events very seriously. By remote control, he raised two more legions in Cisalpine Gaul, and sent to Rome to ask Pompey to lend him one of his. By the end of the winter all three legions were at his headquarters.

He summoned the Gallic chiefs to a conference, but the Senones, Treveri and Carnutes were conspicuous by their absence. They removed their chiefs imposed on them by Caesar. The Senones banished theirs, while only assassination suited the Carnutes. These anti-Roman demonstrations could not be ignored; other tribes looking on might rise up as well, and even the tribes which had submitted to Caesar might review the situation and decide that independence was the better option. Caesar transferred his base to Lutetia (modern Paris) and marched towards the Senones. Without a battle both they and the Carnutes submitted.

The Aedui and the Remi remained firmly with Caesar, which gave him leeway to turn his attention to Ambiorix and the Eburones, and their allies the Menapii and Treveri. Labienus was sent against the latter. He restored Cingetorix to power and overthrew Indutiomarus. Caesar first attacked the Menapii at the mouth of the Rhine, in order to isolate the Eburones by depriving them of allies or refuges. Then when he turned against the Eburones, it was to be no war of pitched battles, Roman army versus tribal warriors; it was a progressive and very thorough wasting of the entire land. Caesar invited the surrounding tribes to join him in pillaging the homesteads of the Eburones, giving them licence to make war on their neighbours by killing, stealing and whatever else they felt might be of advantage. Exploiting inter-tribal rivalries, setting tribe against tribe, was a shameful act of the deepest cynicism; but it was effective. The Eburones were never heard of again, and the fate of Ambiorix is unknown; he was never found, alive or dead.

One of the undesirable results of the invitation to other tribes to help in the destruction of the Eburones was that some of the Sugambri crossed the Rhine to join in, but they diverted and instead attacked the camp at Aduatuca, where Caesar has left Quintus Cicero with the baggage and the Fourteenth legion. The soldiers will have known of the fate of the previous occupants, tricked into leaving by Ambiorix and then massacred. They were very frightened, especially as it was the dreaded Germans who were attacking. They were caught unawares while out foraging, and two cohorts were wiped out. Caesar remarked that it was ironic that the Sugambri had crossed the Rhine to pillage the Eburones, and had unwittingly helped them by attacking the Romans instead. At the next meeting of the Gallic chiefs, who were all summoned to Rheims, Caesar executed Acco, the leader of the Senones, for his part in instigating the disaffection of the tribes. Then with winter approaching, he quartered six out of his ten legions in the lands of the Senones, to watch them and to punish them by the heavy burden of supplying the troops.

Caesar was about to face the most difficult years of the conquest of Gaul. His harshness did not quell the tribes, but inflamed them, not en masse, but some tribes who would not otherwise have worked together now began to think of cooperative action. The moment for the Gallic revolt was propitious. Circumstances in Rome were worsening. Pompey and Caesar were no longer in mutual agreement about their candidates for the consulship of 53, and the elections were delayed. There were riots, and rumours spread that Pompey was to be made Dictator to pacify the city and restore order. He said that he did not desire the office, which was just as well, because Cato made sure that he did not get it.

News arrived in the summer of 53 that Crassus had met with a serious defeat in the east and had been killed. Once again, as with the death of Julia, there is debate as to the effects of Crassus' death on the alliance between Caesar and Pompey. On the whole, his survival may not have influenced events in any way, because the choice for Caesar would still have been to find some means of remaining in office once his proconsulship ended, and he would have had to fight for it by fair means or foul, even if both Pompey and Crassus put their weight behind the scheme. For Pompey, one of his options was to work with Caesar, obtaining his own and Caesar's aims by increasingly uncomfortable, probably illegal measures. He would be gradually overshadowed without military powers, losing his supremacy and independence of action. He would have found himself between a rock and a hard place: he would have to stand alone against Caesar, or ally with the Senate, because there was no other faction. The presence or absence of Crassus would not alter this gradual divergence; the presence of Julia may have delayed the rift, but not averted it.

In 52 the situation degenerated further. Titus Annius Milo was a candidate for the consulship, and Clodius intended to stand for the praetorship, but before the elections were held Clodius was killed by Milo's gang. Deprived of their whimsical benefactor, the people overreacted and used the Senate House as Clodius' funeral pyre. Rome did not possess a standing police force, but it was high time that somebody brought back law and order. Pompey was entrusted with the safety of the state, but not as Dictator, despite appeals that he should be appointed as such. Eventually he was made sole consul, an anomalous and unprecedented situation, since consuls had always come in pairs since the ancient kings had been expelled from Rome.

Caesar's proposed marriage alliance with Pompey, no doubt conveyed via Balbus, was rejected. The plan was for Caesar to divorce his wife Calpurnia and marry Pompey's daughter, and Pompey was to marry Caesar's great niece Octavia, the sister of Octavius, better known to history as Octavian and then Augustus. All this came to nothing, and Pompey eventually married Cornelia, the daughter of Quintus Metellus Scipio, who was noted for his opposition to Caesar. But Pompey was not yet ready to sever all ties with his former colleague, and arranged for Caesar to stand for the consulship of 48 *in absentia*. This would mean that he could remain in his province until 49 and step from proconsulship to consulship unhindered by irritating prosecutions and other nuisances.

This prolongation of his command was for his own political purposes, but in the temporal sphere it was fortuitous that he was to have as free a hand as possible in Transalpine Gaul. Caesar would now need all his resources to fight on two fronts, one in the political arena against his enemies who were determined to bring him down and remove him from his command, and the other in the purely military sense. Until the winter of 53/2 Caesar and the Roman world had only a disinterested acquaintance with a Gallic chief called Vercingetorix.

5 Vercingetorix

When Caesar returned to Gaul at the beginning of 52 the position was probably worse than it had been in 58. Then, he had every prospect of winning over the tribes, installing pro-Roman kings or chiefs, and employing the friendly tribes to keep their neighbours under control. Now, in 52, even the Gauls who had been cooperative and well disposed had begun to turn against Rome. Caesar had cavalierly and cynically exploited inter-tribal rivalries, especially in the destruction of the Eburones; perhaps he thought that these rivalries were insurmountable and the policy of divide and rule would create a system of checks and balances and ensure peace in Gaul. If this was the case, then the revolt proved him wrong. Whilst it was not a complete pan-Gallic rising, it was both widespread and intense.

The opening round was won by the Carnutes, with their massacre of the Roman traders at Cenabum (modern Orleans). It was a major unequivocal statement, addressed both to the Romans and the Gauls, that Roman domination would not be tolerated. Two leaders emerged, Commius of the Gallic Atrebates, and Vercingetorix of the Arverni. Both had been cultivated as friends of the Roman people by Caesar, and both were able to persuade satellite and neighbouring tribes to join them. Caesar's problem was to discern how widespread the revolt was, and how to reach his army. He had only new recruits and a provincial militia at his disposal, and with these he marched towards Narbo (modern Narbonne) immediately after hearing that some tribesmen were closing in on the town. Thus he learned that it was not only the northern parts of Gaul that were under threat but the southern, long-settled parts as well. Vercingetorix was at that moment among the Bituriges, trying to detach them from their connection with the pro-Roman Aedui. Caesar decided to attack the Arverni while their leader was absent, in the expectation that Vercingetorix would return home. He guessed correctly that the Arverni accompanying Vercingetorix would be very agitated about the safety of their homes when they heard that Caesar was approaching their territory. Once he knew that the Gallic leader had been drawn off and was heading for home, Caesar dashed non-stop for the two legions based near Langres, and from there he set about assembling his whole army. He then attacked a settlement of the Senones which he soon took after a brief siege, and

13 Gold coin of Vercingetorix bearing his name. Drawn by Jacqui Taylor

went on to attack Cenabum, where the revolt had started. Then he turned his attention to the Bituriges. Vercingetorix had begun to besiege Gorgobina, a settlement where Caesar had placed the Boii, but he broke off the siege to try to head off Caesar and prevent him from crossing the Loire into the lands of the Bituriges. Caesar was besieging Noviodunum, which was just about to capitulate, but as Vercingetorix approached the occupants were emboldened, and having opened their gates, they closed them again. But Caesar's German cavalry, a legacy from his defeat of Ariovistus, drove off the warriors of Vercingetorix, and Caesar was then free to march on the wealthiest and most important settlement of the Bituriges, Avaricum (modern Bourges).

Knowing that it would be folly to risk a pitched battle, Vercingetorix changed his tactics from open battle to one of attrition, cutting off Caesar's supplies. To this end he ordered his allies either to fortify their towns and prepare for a siege, or if the settlements could not be defended, then they were to burn them along with all food stores and any other supplies that might help the Romans. He was forced to give in when he suggested that it would not be possible to defend Avaricum, since the Bituriges were unwilling to sacrifice it. Otherwise they cooperated with Vercingetorix; they burnt 20 settlements in one day, according to Caesar. The leadership of Vercingetorix was a new phenomenon. He inspired such confidence in himself and the possibility of success that he was able to unite several tribes under one supreme chief and was then able to persuade them to take this drastic step of destroying their homes to deny the Romans any benefits from them. The Gauls had seen the Romans in action, and that gave them the incentive to sink their differences and fight together for their survival and freedom.

It is significant that though the Aedui and the Remi remained loyal to Caesar, the tribes in revolt did not consider the option of submitting to him before they joined Vercingetorix. Friendship with the Romans gave a notional freedom, and could bring material benefits, but it was not freedom as the Gauls knew it.

The new policy of Vercingetorix put Caesar's army under stress. When food supplies ran low at Avaricum, Caesar suggested that he should break off the siege, but as he records in his account of the war the soldiers would not hear of it. Stalemate set in. Caesar had not reduced Avaricum, and when Vercingetorix camped nearby the defences of his camp proved too strong for the Romans when they attacked by night, hoping to take advantage of the temporary absence of the Gallic leader. When Vercingetorix returned, the Gauls were very shaken, but he turned their complaints about the lack of an appointed deputy to an accolade when he insisted that the Romans were terrified and that was why they had broken off the attack.

Meanwhile Caesar was building a ramp to reach the defences of Avaricum. It presumably contained a framework of timber, since the Gauls were able to set it alight from a mine shaft that they had sunk underneath it. The troops that Caesar had posted on permanent guard duty were able to cut a fire break, and beat off the Gauls who rushed out of the gates to the attack. From inside the town the defenders threw pitch and grease, and anything that would ignite, onto the ramp so that it would burn more thoroughly. The fighting was prolonged, and next day Caesar noted the determination and bravery of the Gauls on the ramparts, throwing balls of pitch. One man was killed by Roman missiles, and another stepped into his place, until he too was killed, and so on, one man after another, until the fighting ceased. In his writing for public consumption, Caesar was impressed with the pertinacity and self-sacrifice of the Gauls, and privately, while he watched these events, perhaps he appreciated for the first time the depth of the extreme hatred of Roman rule. He preached the benefits of friendship with Rome, and may even have been possessed of a missionary zeal that prevented him from grasping that there were people who preferred their own way of life to what he considered to be the superior material and social advantages of Roman civilisation.

Avaricum fell in the end, on a day of heavy rain, when the ramparts were not strongly defended and the Roman siege towers could be pushed close to the walls. The Romans exacted revenge for the massacre of the traders and merchants at Cenabum, by a corresponding massacre of the inhabitants of Avaricum, including the women and children. A lesser man than Vercingetorix would have crumbled, but by force of personality he was able to retain and even increase the faith that the Gauls invested in him. Instead of losing adherents after the Roman massacre of the Gauls at Avaricum, he gained more. It was disquieting for Caesar that the loyal Aedui were now beginning to waver. They had never been wholly united in friendship with Rome, and there was a danger that the anti-Roman party that was growing in strength would finally persuade the rest to throw in their lot with Vercingetorix. Caesar spent valuable time on public relations, bringing the Aedui back to their alliance. It was of vital importance to him since he wished to use their territory as a base, and to be able to rely upon the tribe to supply his army.

Besides the host gathered by Vercingetorix, there were additional threats to the north from the Senones and Parisi. Caesar divided his forces, sending Titus Labienus northwards with four legions while he himself took the rest of the army and aimed for Gergovia, the chief settlement of the Arverni. To reach it he had to cross the river Allier to its western bank. Vercingetorix shadowed him as he marched and destroyed all the bridges, but this did not prevent Caesar from crossing the river. When he learned that the Romans had crossed the Allier, Vercingetorix dashed straight for Gergovia to reach it before Caesar. It was a naturally strong settlement on a high plateau. On the southern edge of the town Vercingetorix built a camp protected by a dry stone wall, and garrisoned a nearby hill, nowadays called Le Roche Blanche, to secure the water supply and the pasture. It was this area that Caesar decided to attack, since one look at the place was enough to convince him that he could not take Gergovia by force. He encamped and then set about taking La Roche Blanche. He built a smaller camp to the south-east of the town, took the hill by night, placed two legions on it and joined the small camp to the large one by two parallel ditches.

At this point, trouble erupted among the Aedui. One of the chiefs of the loyal Aeduans who were with Caesar, a man called Eporedorix, reported to him that he had heard that a faction of his tribe led by Litaviccus had spread the rumour that all the Aeduans in Caesar's army, including the two chiefs Eporedorix and Viridomarus, had been accused of treachery and massacred. The tribesmen had killed all the Romans in charge of one of the supply convoys, and were probably massing under the leadership of Litaviccus, ready to march on Caesar's camp. Without delay, Caesar mobilised, leaving a small garrison to hold the camps at Gergovia. About 25 miles from the town he met Litaviccus and the rebel Aeduans. There was no battle because the two leaders Eporedorix and Viridomarus were patently not dead, so the tribesmen now knew that Litaviccus had stirred up trouble under false pretences. They surrendered. Caesar left it at that, notifying the Aedui that he could have executed all the nobles, but had decided against it. He was anxious to waste no time in returning to Gergovia. He allowed the soldiers a short

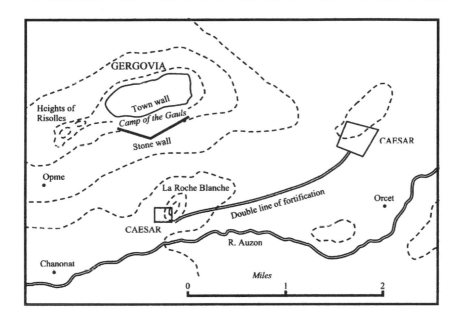

14 *The siege of Gergovia. The town was situated on a plateau at the summit of a mountain 1,200ft above sea level, with steep slopes on the northern and eastern sides. The town had a defensive wall on the southern side where the slopes were less steep. This was where Vercingetorix made his camp, building another stone wall in front of the town. Caesar's first camp was laid out to the south-east, then he took the heights to the south, built a second camp and linked both camps by means of two communication trenches, 12ft wide. After an assault which failed, Caesar was forced to move off into the territory of the Aedui.* Drawn by Jan Shearsmith

rest, then marched them back, hastening when he heard that in his absence the Gauls had attacked his camp.

There were no serious consequences, but Caesar knew that he would have to give up the attempt to take Gergovia. Before he left he determined to gain at least something from the blockade. The hill to the south-west of Gergovia was the key to the assault. First Caesar drew off the defenders to this unprotected point by pretending that he was going to attack there. He put his baggage men on their mules as fake cavalry, and sent a legion towards the hill, then when the Gauls were preparing for battle he suddenly launched an attack on the camp that Vercingetorix had built to the south of the town. According to Caesar, the original plan was to pull back once the damage had been done and the score was settled, but in their ardour the troops pressed on, oblivious of the signals to retreat. They forced their way through the camp until they came up against the town defences, where they met such fierce opposition that they were stopped in their tracks. The cost was high: 700 soldiers and 46 centurions dead, and many wounded. The story about the planned retreat sounds a little like a cover-up for an assault that went wrong. Knowing his men, Caesar rectified the situation by drawing up the whole army in battle formation the next morning. He praised them for their zeal, but emphasised that discipline was also important. The whole parade was for display and the restoration of morale, since there was no chance that Vercingetorix would bring his warriors out of the stronghold to take up the offer of battle.

The scene now shifted to Noviodunum on the lands of the Aedui. It was Caesar's headquarters and administrative centre, and therefore a natural focal point for the persistent rebel Aeduans to attack. Eporedorix and Viridomarus changed sides without warning, and ordered the tribesmen to kill the soldiers and all the traders, and to destroy the food stores. The whole area was roused against the Romans. Caesar was now almost boxed in by hostile Gauls. He badly needed to unite his army, so he marched to join Labienus. This entailed crossing the Loire, but he moved so rapidly that he met with no opposition. Labienus was informed that Caesar had failed at Gergovia, and had fallen back to the Roman Province in the south, so as far as he knew he was cut off and Caesar was miles away. Undaunted, he started to march south with his four legions, outwitting the Gauls who tried to stop him from crossing the Seine. Disaster was avoided and the two armies met up, but the situation of the united Roman army was far from safe. The supply problem was only one of the difficulties. The defection of the Aedui was a bitter blow, especially since Caesar had spent so much time and effort on cultivating them. The Remi, however, held firm, and Vercingetorix failed in his attempt to win them over. Likewise the Lingones, and the Allobroges of southern Gaul, refused to renounce their Roman alliance. There was also a slight rift in the Gallic camp, since the Aedui wished to direct operations, so Vercingetorix had to assert his authority. The tribesmen voted in favour of him as leader, and he persuaded them that his policy of starving the Romans out was the correct one.

There would be no swift, sharp victories for the Gauls because they knew that the Romans could go on recruiting soldiers almost indefinitely, bringing armies into Gaul under any number of commanders to avenge themselves if they had suffered defeats. The main hope for the Gallic army was to avoid pitched battles, to attack on a small scale whenever there was an opportunity, wearing down Caesar's army by guerrilla tactics and denying them supplies, and waiting. The Gauls would attend closely to the political developments in Rome, where there was a growing anti-Caesarian lobby, not yet powerful, but perhaps one day soon it would be powerful enough to topple Caesar from his command. If not, then it would surely expire and Caesar would return to Rome. Another winter might see the end of him in Gaul.

Vercingetorix moved his headquarters to Alesia in the territory of the Mandubii. He encouraged the Aedui and other tribes to attack the Province, and in response Caesar appointed a relative of his, Lucius Caesar, to attend to its defence. Twenty-two cohorts were recruited and strung out along the borders of the Province, and the Allobroges blocked the passage of the attacking Gauls across the Rhine. This was an inadequate defence, as Caesar well knew, but his troops could do nothing without rest, he was cut off from Italy, and he needed reinforcements. He sent for contingents of German horsemen from the tribes across the Rhine, but when they arrived he found their horses unsuitable, and to remedy the defects he made his officers give up their riding horses for use as cavalry mounts. Then he set out for the Province, through the lands of the Sequani.

Vercingetorix advanced from Alesia, hoping to surprise Caesar on the march. His plan was to place his infantry in battle order in front of his encampment and send the cavalry to attack the head and flanks of the marching column. It seems that Caesar was not aware of the presence of the Gauls, and the plan had every chance of success, but the Gallic cavalry attack did not have sufficient initial impetus to roll the column back. That short delay allowed Caesar time to assess the situation, bring up his own cavalry to hold off the Gauls, and order his legions to form squares with the baggage in the centre. Details are lacking in Caesar's history about this battle. The Romans won in the end so he did not need to be coy about describing what happened. Perhaps there was more confusion and panic than he was prepared to admit, and in any case he ought to have been prepared for an attack, covering himself by sending out scouts to reconnoitre the road ahead of his troops.

Vercingetorix withdrew into Alesia, where he made a camp and began to fortify the weakest parts of the stronghold. The settlement lies on a plateau surrounded on three sides by rivers, the Ose and Oserain to the north and south, both flowing into the river Brenne on the western side. When Caesar arrived, he reconnoitred and concluded, as at Gergovia, that a siege was not a viable option, so a long blockade was the only choice available. He started to encircle the whole area with banks and ditches, distributing the troops in camps along the fortifications. Before he had fully completed the works, Vercingetorix attacked Caesar's cavalry on the west side of the town. The battle was going badly for the Romans until Caesar sent in the German horsemen. The Gauls turned and made for their camp, but they could not ride in through the gates quickly enough, and had to stand and fight. For the German cavalry, it was not a

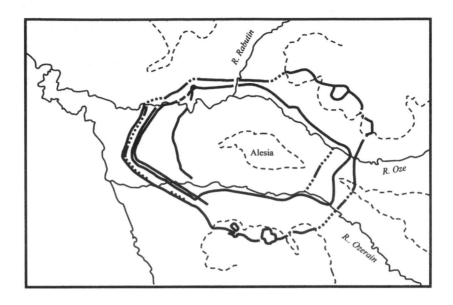

15 The siege of Alesia. Vercingetorix withdrew his whole army to Alesia after he tried and failed to annihilate Caesar's army on the march. The town was not as elevated as Gergovia, but still well protected by the sloping ground all around it. Caesar decided to blockade the place rather than besiege it, and set about enclosing it within extended lines of siege works, but there was also the problem that he might be attacked by a relieving army, and therefore he had to build defensive works facing outwards in addition to those facing inwards. Drawn by Jan Shearsmith

battle but a slaughter. The Gauls then tried to escape up the hill towards the town but Vercingetorix ordered all the gates to be shut.

The defeat seems to have shaken him. Instead of using his horsemen to keep on breaking out to harass the Romans, Vercingetorix decided to bottle himself up inside the defences, sending all his horsemen away during the night, with orders to go home and recruit more tribesmen to come to the aid of those left at Alesia. The absence of the horses would ease the problem of supplies to feed them, but he left himself without the means of offensive defence. As for supplies for the warriors, he reckoned that he could last out for about a month, and immediately started to ration food. Caesar heard of this from deserters and immediately applied himself to tightening the cordon around the town, and to protecting himself from external attack by the relieving force that was bound to appear sooner or later. This entailed building two sets of defences, one facing inwards and the other outwards. The outer line was 14 miles in extent.

If the blockaded Gauls were short of supplies Caesar's situation was little better. He had many mouths to feed — his army has been estimated at 70,000 men — and he needed reserves as well as daily supplies to prepare for the probability that eventually he would be cut off from the countryside, which was in any case quite barren for a considerable radius after only one or two days. Foraging was an increasingly time-consuming and difficult operation, taking the horsemen further and further away on each expedition, but the one consolation was that Vercingetorix evidently had no intention of attacking the foraging parties.

Meanwhile a huge army of Gauls was assembling to relieve Alesia. The Aeduans contributed about 250,000 infantry, led by their chiefs Eporedorix and Viridomarus, and a relative of Vercingetorix called Vercassivellaunus. Among the other leaders was Caesar's former ally, the chief of the Atrebates, Commius. This army, together with warriors and horsemen from many other tribes, set out for Alesia, and once there, occupied the high ground to the west of the beleaguered town. Next day they brought the cavalry down into the plain to face Caesar's outer defence works. At the same time the Gauls in Alesia attacked the inner defence works, suggesting that there was communication between the two Gallic armies. Caesar manned both lines and sent out his cavalry to engage the enemy. The battle lasted all afternoon until evening, and once again it was the German horsemen who scattered the Gauls of the relieving force. As these sped back to their camp on the heights, Vercingetorix withdrew his men from the inner lines and retired.

The next attack was by night, again from both sides of Caesar's lines, but they were not breached. The Gauls had observed that to the north of the town, where the river Rabutin joined the Ose, the outer Roman lines were not joined up. Two legions guarded this spot. This was chosen as the focal point for the next attack. The relieving army marched round to the north, while from inside Vercingetorix mounted a number of assaults at different points to ensure that the Romans could not leave their defences to mass at one threatened point. Caesar had to take command himself at one point where the Gauls had reached the defences of the inner line and begun to tear them down. Labienus and six cohorts were sent to the aid of the two legions guarding the gap in the outer line, where the Gallic relieving force was now pressing their attack home. He too was soon in difficulties, so Caesar gathered some cavalry and infantry and set off to join Labienus. As a safeguard he sent another force round the outside to come up behind the Gauls. This attack from the rear surprised and disconcerted the Gauls, and especially when they recognised Caesar's red cloak, the badge of Roman commanders, they began to falter. This may be pure Caesarian rhetoric, of course, to paint himself in heroic colours, but whether it was due to his presence the tide turned in favour of the Romans. The Gauls were heavily defeated, and so many were killed that it was decided to abandon the camp. The Romans pursued, killing all the way. It signified the end of any attempt to relieve Alesia.

There was no longer any hope of victory or even survival for Vercingetorix and the Gauls of Alesia. There was no time to raise another relief army before the food ran out. Vercingetorix assembled his chiefs and offered to surrender himself to the Romans. Caesar was informed, and prepared to receive the Gallic leaders next day. He demanded the surrender of all weapons. Vercingetorix rode in, dismounted, and knelt before Caesar. It is one of the most moving moments of history. The man who had for a brief few months nearly united the Gauls into nationhood, and who stood for freedom against the Roman Imperialist advance, acknowledged failure and sacrificed himself for his people. The concept of a nation of Gauls was too revolutionary for the tribes under the command of Vercingetorix. It could have had only a brief shelf-life before tribal loyalties superseded Gallic loyalties. Vercingetorix' policy of guerrilla warfare, patience and waiting, could have won the war in the end, but the promised rewards of freedom from Roman domination were too far off, uncertain and nebulous. Immediate success might have welded the Gauls together, but what was lacking was the temptation of personal wealth and power at the end of the road. Caesar had the edge because his legions could look forward to pay and rewards; pay days were probably sporadic, but the soldiers had enough faith in Caesar to know that he would not let them down, and there was the prospect of booty as well as fame and glory. Vercingetorix could offer nothing like this, only hardship and years of recovery afterwards, hunger, and perhaps death for a cause. Noble sentiments, certainly, but lacking the pulling power of sackloads of ready cash.

Vercingetorix could have chosen to flee from Alesia if he could, and continue to fight somewhere else. He could have died gloriously in battle, or perhaps at the hand of another Gallic chief who saw a quick way of bringing the war to an end. As it was, he waited for six years in a Roman prison, walked behind Caesar's chariot in one of his triumphs, and was then strangled. When his country became a nation, he became a national hero, as the gigantic statue at Alise Sainte-Reine attests.

The fall of Alesia did not signify the end of the revolt. Caesar went some way to diffuse opposition by a reversal of his hitherto merciless policy. He returned his Aeduan and Arvernian prisoners to their tribes, and allowed the Aedui to resume their former status as friends of the Roman people, and he left their internal organisation untouched. He put his troops into winter quarters, and remained at Bibracte in Aeduan territory, anticipating further trouble. The Bituriges obliged at the beginning of 51, and Caesar marched against them, leaving one of his young commanders in charge of the winter camp, an officer called

Marcus Antonius, or Mark Antony, who had been with Caesar for some time, but without mention in the history of the Gallic war until the description of its later stages.

The Bituriges were defeated, but once again Caesar did not resort to harsh treatment. He demanded hostages but did not take bloody revenge, perhaps counting upon leniency to persuade the Gauls that there was more to be gained by cooperation with Rome than by risking a battle against his armies. As resistance fell away the tribes started to fight each other. The Carnutes raided the Bituriges, and Commius the arch rebel and dedicated survivor encouraged the Bellovaci to attack the Suessiones. Caesar repulsed the attacks in both cases; the Bituriges were commanded by Correus and Commius, and it required an energetic campaign to reduce them. Correus encamped on high ground in the forest of Compiègne, and Caesar came up to make camp opposite him. There were a few skirmishes, and the Bituriges gained the edge when Commius brought in some 500 German horsemen, whose fighting qualities Caesar had recognised and used to good effect. Caesar started to enclose the camp of the Bituriges, who saw clearly the parallel with Alesia, and made efforts to get away. They did so eventually, by retreating behind a massive smoke and fire screen at night. The scene shifted to another camp from which Correus raided the Roman foraging parties. Caesar determined to catch them at their own game, and sent out a forage party accompanied by infantry and cavalry hidden from view. When the Gauls attacked, the Romans counter-attacked, and the victory shattered resistance. Once more Caesar treated the tribesmen leniently, instead of exacting terrible revenge. It was a calculated policy, and it paid off, because other tribes submitted to him voluntarily.

Commius was still at large, and could not be allowed to remain so because of his anti-Roman fanaticism. He may have been the prime force behind the other chiefs who determined to resist the Romans. The name of Ambiorix surfaced from time to time, and stiffened the resolve of the tribes to fight, so in savage response Caesar went through what was left of Ambiorix' tribe, the Eburones, with fire and sword. His policy of leniency did not apply in this part of the world, perhaps because Caesar saw no profit in it. Labienus was sent against the Treveri, and other officers were sent on operations in the north-west of Gaul. Caesar felt secure enough to despatch one legion to Cisalpine Gaul, ostensibly to guard against an incursion into Illyricum, but in reality to make a political statement to his enemies in Rome who were agitating for his recall.

There was little time left now to consolidate his gains and pacify the country before Caesar's term as governor expired. The controversy over when precisely this was meant to be has caused much ink to flow without resolving the problem beyond informed speculation. In broad general terms, Caesar wanted the consulship of 48 without standing down to go to Rome for the elections, which meant that he had to remain in Gaul and in command of troops until the elections of 49. The question is whether this was perfectly legal and condoned in Rome, and if not, how far was he stretching the point. With regard to Gaul, no matter what the precise date was when he should give up his command, he had little time and consequently little patience with the tribesmen who breathed life into the last embers of the revolt. Two leaders called Drappes and Lucterius occupied Uxellodunum (modern Puy d'Issolu), where they had amassed quantities of food and stores to last them and their army through a siege, hoping no doubt that Caesar would be recalled to Rome and another commander would perhaps prove less intransigent than the last one. The one vital element that the Gauls were unable to protect or to store was water. When Caesar arrived in person he set his engineers on the task of cutting off the water supply, and the inevitable consequence was the surrender of Uxellodunum. On this occasion Caesar acted more ruthlessly than ever before, bringing an end to the war but little credit to himself, at least in modern eyes. He lined up all the men who had taken up arms against him, and cut off their hands. Killing them was not memorable enough, because he had seen how readily the Gauls died in battle or for a cause. He wanted the survivors to remain as visible reminders of the power of Rome, *pour encourager les autres* as the modern descendants of the Gauls would say.

The last of the Gauls to surrender was Commius. He gave himself up to Mark Antony. Organisation of the country could begin. Most of Gaul was exhausted, some of the land completely wasted or pillaged out of existence, some of it resettled by tribes who hailed from other parts of Gaul. It was time to establish tribal boundaries, recognising each one as a different state, organising its relations with Rome, and assessing the tribute to be paid. Common sense ruled, instead of Imperialist greed. The Gauls could not pay fantastic sums from their devastated lands, so Caesar settled for a total of 10 million denarii, a sum that he or any Roman aristocrat could probably have matched from his personal fortune several times over. The organisation of Gaul involved Caesar in a great deal of personal negotiation, promoting chiefs who were well disposed to Rome, sending lavish gifts to keep them loyal, all with the tacit understanding that Roman armed support would be forthcoming at the least sign of trouble, the corollary of course being that armed Roman persuasion would also be forthcoming at the least sign of disloyalty. It was of the utmost importance to Caesar to avoid any further outbreaks of fighting so near to the end of his governorship. That would have diverted his attention and that of his loyal army from his next project, which was the political conquest of Rome.

6 'They would have it so': the road to Pharsalus

One of the most tantalising problems concerning Caesar's command in Gaul, as mentioned above, is the lack of clarity about the date when it expired. The initial law bestowing the command of Cisalpine Gaul and Illyricum on Caesar was passed by the tribune Publius Vatinius, who went directly to the popular assembly to pass his law. The *lex Vatinia* gave Caesar a command of five years, and in order to avoid forcible replacement, such as had happened to Lucullus in the east, the law stipulated that there should be no discussion of recalling Caesar until 1 March 54. His command of Transalpine Gaul was for one year initially, renewable annually. Pompey and Crassus as consuls for 55 confirmed Caesar's command, presumably unifying the two separate components, and extended it for a further five years. It is still not certain whether a specific terminal date was set for the command, and if so, what date that was. The extension of five years may have been intended to pick up where the *lex Vatinia* left off, that is from 2 March 54, in which case it should terminate in March 49, or it may have been dated from the *lex Trebonia* of November 55 which conferred on Pompey and Crassus their provincial commands until 1 March 50. This is the date that Pompey endorsed when pressure to recall Caesar was mounting.

The duration of Caesar's command and the feasibility of his recall came under the scrutiny of one of the consuls for 51, Marcus Claudius Marcellus, a confirmed and bitter anti-Caesarian. The point at issue was not the command itself nor its duration, but the fact that the enemies of Caesar, and probably not a few whose sympathies were more neutral, did not on any account want Caesar as consul in 48, or in any other year, for a repeat of the fun and frolics of 59. In order to prevent his election his enemies had to divest him of his proconsulship and find some means of bringing him down before he could be elected to any magistracy, otherwise he would be immune to any prosecution if he passed directly from proconsul to consul.

Marcellus played on the reports of the victory at Alesia, suggesting that the Gallic war was over and a new governor should be sent out immediately. This was a genuine possibility, because of the legislation that Pompey had passed while he was sole consul in 52. The *lex Pompeia de provinciis* established the rule that there must be a five-year interval between a magistracy and a promagistracy, or an office held at Rome and a post as governor of a province. It created an immediate shortfall in personnel, since none of the magistrates of 52 could proceed to a province when his office came to an end. In order to fill the gap, those men who had held offices but who had not been particularly ambitious to govern a province now had to be coerced. One of the casualties was Cicero who had to go out to Cilicia as its governor, much against the grain, because to Cicero the centre of the universe, and therefore of his existence, was Rome. Technically this law also made it possible to send out a replacement for Caesar in Gaul because there would be no need to wait until the magistrates of 49 had completed their term of office; there would be other ex-consulars who would be eligible, and the precedent was set of choosing men who had not angled for important commands. True, this had always been the case, that there were candidates in Rome to send out to Gaul, but Pompey's law now highlighted the possibility.

The other law that Pompey passed while he was sole consul was the *lex Pompeia de iure magistratuum*, requiring candidates to present themselves in person for the elections. At first sight it seems that Pompey had deliberately turned against Caesar by making it impossible for him to remain in Gaul until he was elected consul, but in reality he honoured the law of the Ten Tribunes that specifically allowed Caesar to stand *in absentia* for the consular elections. The Pompeian law was not aimed at Caesar himself, but it was designed to prevent others from forming the habit of standing for office whilst not actually in Rome; in other words, Caesar was a special case and was also the last. As for replacing Caesar immediately, Pompey inserted a clause into the *lex Pompeia de provinciis* exempting Caesar. He has been accused by modern authors of everything from guile to forgetfulness, but all he was doing was tightening up the loopholes that enabled Caesar to further his career, without undue prejudice to him. It was unfair to those who came after Caesar, but fairness was the very last descriptive term that anyone could apply to Roman politics. It cannot be said that Pompey had definitively broken with Caesar and joined the opposition at this stage in the proceedings. Pompey was and always had been a law unto himself and not a mouthpiece for the Senate, and he was neither pro-Caesarian nor the head of an anti-Caesarian party. Whenever he was approached about the recall of Caesar, he upheld the regulation that Caesar's command was not to be discussed until after 1 March 50. He was cautious in order to avoid becoming embroiled in a situation that he could not escape from, or direct to his satisfaction.

As the Gallic war came to an end, Caesar began to write his account of it in 51. One of his officers, Aulus Hirtius, completed the work, no doubt from notes left by Caesar, perhaps compiled while on campaign. Caesar had sent regular reports back to the Senate about each stage of the wars, and the fact that names of officers are recorded whenever they performed heroic deeds indicates that the reports were written up soon after the events. The work would appeal to the loyalty of the army to its commander, since units and individuals were mentioned, and it also contributed to the propaganda that Caesar wished to spread about his worthy achievements on behalf of Rome. It was part of the system to court voters and inform them of the value of their prospective consul for 48.

In the same spirit of gaining clients and support at the polls, Caesar fostered the Gauls of northern Italy. He had recruited legionaries in Cisalpine Gaul as though the people were already citizens of Rome, and he had settled veterans at Novum Comum as colonists with Roman citizenship. Marcellus tried to divest these colonists of their citizenship, but Caesar's tribunes vetoed the suggestion. Relenting for a while, Marcellus next seized a citizen of Comum and had him flogged; Roman citizens were supposed to be immune from this sort of punishment, and Marcellus used the unfortunate individual in order to provoke Caesar. Perhaps he had forgotten that Pompey's family also had considerable interest in the Gauls of northern Italy, having bestowed upon them partial citizenship, a halfway stage to full citizenship. As the Gallic war wound down, Caesar detached one legion and posted it in Cisalpine Gaul. He gave out that he wished to guard against an invasion from Illyricum, but the move also proclaimed that Caesar would not hesitate to use his army to ward off political attacks upon him. Pompey was asked what he would do if Caesar tried to keep his army and also become consul, and he dismissed the idea as preposterous, with the famous phrase 'What if my son should beat me with a stick?'. No one thought to point out that Pompey had already set the precedent by holding office as consul and also governor of Spain with access to troops.

Having survived the consulship of Marcus Marcellus, Caesar was still under threat from the consuls of 50, Gaius Claudius Marcellus, a relative of the consul of 51, and Lucius Aemilius Paullus. Both of them were hostile to Caesar. Fortunately, most of the tribunes were Caesarians, except for Gaius Scribonius Curio, whose track record so far was wholly anti-Caesar. In order to change people's allegiances, Caesar successfully employed that old instrument of persuasion, hard cash. The campaigns in Gaul had filled his coffers with unimaginable wealth, which he had been distributing freely since 58 to buy people and to continue to support them and his friends. Now he used money to neutralise Aemilius Paullus and more important to bring Curio over to his own camp. Curio was a friend of Mark Antony, and the two of them had enjoyed a roisterous youth, with mounting debts that Caesar presumably settled for both of them, while promising still more. Curio seems to have suffered no pangs of conscience about changing sides so decisively. From 50 onwards he did Caesar brilliant service. When discussions began in March about the recall of Caesar, he vetoed everything that would have been detrimental to his patron, and he kept it up for two months. The consul Gaius Marcellus proposed that Caesar should now be replaced without delay, Curio innocently countered with another proposal that Pompey and Caesar should both lay down their commands simultaneously. He had obviously been primed by Caesar, who understood the immense popular appeal of such a proposal. Indeed both senators and people favoured it, so it cast a churlish light on Pompey when he refused, while Caesar lost nothing and even gained approval.

Shortly afterwards Caesar was manoeuvred into giving up two legions. Reports reached Rome that the Parthians were fomenting trouble in the east with designs on Syria, where Marcus Calpurnius Bibulus was currently governor. He would need reinforcements, so Pompey announced that both he and Caesar would contribute one legion, then promptly designated his legion as the one he had lent to Caesar in 53. He was perfectly within his rights, and if Caesar refused he would seem to be acting against the interests of Rome. Deprived of the physical presence of the two legions, Caesar made sure that he gained some use out of them for propaganda purposes, priming the officers to spread the false but credible rumour that the whole army in Gaul was disaffected and would come over to Pompey once they set foot in Italy. In order to ensure that the soldiers remembered him at least in the short term, Caesar gave the soldiers 250 drachmas each.

In December 50, Curio would cease to be tribune, so someone must be found who could continue to work in Caesar's favour. Mark Antony was the favoured candidate, and so travelled to Rome for the elections. He also decided to stand for appointment as augur, since the death of the orator Hortensius created a vacancy in the college that must be filled. It was a useful appointment, since one of the duties of the augurs was to watch the skies and specifically the flight of birds for omens, and if they were unfavourable all business could be stopped. Caesar might one day find this a useful political tool, and Antony would need only a hint to come up with the required pronouncement.

Antony gained his tribuneship, not least because the people preferred him to the rabid anti-Caesarian Lucius Domitius Ahenobarbus, but Caesar was not successful with his consular candidate, Servius Sulpicius Galba, who was defeated in the elections in the summer of 50 for the consulship of 49. Lucius Lentulus and Gaius Marcellus, the son of Marcus Marcellus, were elected instead. Curio proposed over and over again that Pompey and Caesar should simultaneously lay down their commands, and just before his term of office was about to expire on 9 December, he put the proposal to the vote on 1 December. The senators voted 320 to 22 in favour of the proposal, but it was not adopted, on the grounds that it would involve a complete surrender to Caesar. The consul Marcellus precipitated matters, taking the law into his own hands by entrusting Pompey with the defence of the state. Pompey accepted. He had formed an erroneous impression of the support that he enjoyed in Italy, partly because after his long illness in the spring the rejoicing at his recovery was tremendous, and he thought that he could raise troops very quickly — he said that he only had to stamp his foot in Italy and troops would rise up.

Caesar had played the game more or less according to the rules so far, especially since he had repeatedly offered to lay down his command if Pompey did the same. Pompey's position was anomalous, and it gave Caesar enough leeway to use the anomaly to promote his own cause; either he should be treated in the same way and allowed to keep his army to equal Pompey, or if he had to surrender his army then Pompey should be treated in the same way and made to give up his, so that neither one of them could emerge more powerful than the other. From Caesar's official standpoint, his electoral manifesto almost, his proposal was a simple equation, one that met with popular and senatorial favour, and only the intransigence of a small party in the Senate prevented it from being adopted. He had been patient so far; now he hardened. He sent a message to the Senate via Curio that he would not lay down his command unless Pompey did the same. This was subtly different from the proposal that both should lay down their commands at the same time; that was an offer, a sensible way out of the situation, whereas this was a declaration with no chance of negotiation. It was the turning point, more decisive than crossing the Rubicon. It shifted the focus from the Senate, Cato and the rest to Pompey himself, who up to now was not the real enemy. The responsibility for what happened next could no longer be blamed on the state system or the political set up; everything now depended on Pompey himself. He was backed into a corner where he would have to do something. Effectively, Caesar had portrayed him as the sole obstacle to peace, as the oppressor, as the one who was out of line. Pompey had only a few choices, of backing down and becoming a private citizen, of joining with Caesar as his ally and hoping to emerge with some power and dignity, of facing Caesar alone, or of allying with the Senate and taking the lead. He had already begun to incline in that direction, but not wholeheartedly. He may have considered removing himself from Rome and going to Spain, with another long term as governor, and at one point he told Cicero that he was to go there, but all he would be able to achieve would be a postponement of the current situation with a role reversal, Pompey playing the part of Caesar returning home from the province, to face Caesar in Pompey's position in Rome, by then infinitely stronger.

The option that he did not consider was giving up his army and stepping down. He would have been rapidly overshadowed by Caesar and out of his depth in the political arena. Pompey always needed to save Rome from a dire threat and then come home to adulation and praise. With Caesar in Rome or out of it in a position of power and influence, he could be sure that the credit would be diverted or diluted. Caesar did not for one moment imagine that Pompey would choose this option and would have been disconcerted if he had done so. Then he would have had to concentrate on the opposition of the Senate, without the convenient focal point and single obstacle represented by Pompey. Converting Pompey into the enemy diverted attention away from the fact that what Caesar really had to fight to promote his career was the entire system, the law, hallowed custom, and tradition. Even supposing, in a fantasy world, that Pompey had stood down and the Senate had acquiesced in allowing Caesar to become consul, he had only one year in which to achieve anything, probably in the teeth of opposition from his colleague and from the tribunes. What would he have aimed for next? Several men had reached a second consulship; several had governed more than one province. He could have led an expedition to Dacia; there was distinction in that, but it was all on the same basis as Britain and Gaul, and though it would give him honours and prestige, it would not bestow on him executive power. Caesar thought in terms of the whole Roman world, not yet an Empire by name; he thought in broad, sweeping, long-lasting terms, not puny annual steps in Rome; he was brimming with common-sense ideas and grandiose plans that brooked no opposition, and he was not a young man any longer. Caesar wanted more than the system could give him, and so he had to change the system.

When Caesar's message was read out in the Senate, declaring that he would not give up his army unless Pompey did so as well, the consul forbade any vote on the issue. Instead, after some debate, Metellus Scipio, Pompey's father-in-law, and his consular colleague for what remained of the year 52 when Pompey was sole consul, proposed that a date should be fixed when Caesar should terminate his command. If he refused to comply, then he should be declared an enemy of the state. The subtext was that if Caesar wanted the consulship then he must come to Rome and stand as a candidate without his army at his beck and call, the position that he had struggled all along to avoid. The tribunes Antony and Cassius vetoed the proposal. Debate continued for a few days.

Cicero, just returned from his province, tried to arbitrate and failed. It seemed that no compromise was possible. There was a suggestion that Caesar should be allowed to keep the province of Illyricum with one legion, but when Pompey seemed ready to accept it, Cato whipped up opposition. The Senate passed the ultimate decree, authorising the consuls and magistrates to protect the state. This negated the veto of the tribunes, but when Antony and Cassius protested that they were supposed to be inviolate, they were thrown out of the Senate and told not to return if they wished to avoid violence. The starting flag had been dropped. Antony and Cassius, together with Curio and Caelius, all fled to Caesar, who was now officially declared an enemy of the state. The civil war had begun, whether Caesar crossed the Rubicon or not.

An expert psychologist and manipulator, Caesar presented the two tribunes to the soldiers, just as they were, weary and unwashed. They were supposed to be inviolate, and this was how the Senate had treated them. And the commander, who had conquered Gaul, and done everything for Rome, was now an enemy of the state, an outlaw, denied the use of fire and water, at the mercy of anyone who wished to kill him with impunity. That implied that the soldiers, who had also gone through all those hardships for Rome, were also enemies of the state. That was how the Senate rewarded them. Caesar was able to wring every last drop of propaganda out of the appearance of Antony and Cassius at his camp.

He did not intend to sit and wait to be attacked. He had only one legion with him; the rest of his legions were still in Gaul, but he could not afford to wait for the whole army to join him, since that would give the Senate and Pompey time to mobilise. Despite his lack of troops, Caesar hesitated only briefly on the night of 10/11 January before he marched across the boundary between Cisalpine Gaul and Italy, the river Rubicon. It was not a tremendous physical obstacle like the Rhine, but as a psychological barrier it was enormous, because on the Italian side of the river Caesar was converted from provincial governor to a Roman general making war on Romans.

In effect there was little enough for Pompey to mobilise. The Senate perhaps believed that Caesar's army really would come over to Pompey when the soldiers arrived in Italy, or if they would not go so far then it might be possible that Caesar would have difficulty in persuading them to follow him in a civil war. The Senate perhaps imagined that Pompey was ready to face Caesar, but the reality was very different. Two of Pompey's legions had been with Caesar in Gaul, and though one of them had started out as Pompey's own, the loyalty of the two legions was suspect. The total of the Pompeian legions is not clear. He said he had ten altogether, but that total probably included the troops in Spain. The simple truth was that Pompey was not ready, and he knew it.

Caesar advanced rapidly, seizing important towns on the way. By the first morning in Italy he had taken Ariminum. Antony with five cohorts occupied Arretium, and Curio with four cohorts took Iguvium, where the Pompeian troops put up no resistance and went home. Caesar includes in his history of the civil war a story that Pompey sent a message to him to explain that he had no choice except to act as he did, and asked, more or less, that there should be no hard feelings between them. There may have been more on offer in the message than Caesar mentions; at any rate he replied as he had always replied, that he would give up his army if Pompey would do the same and go to Spain, then he would come to Rome to stand for the consulship. But it was too late for negotiation, because no one trusted anyone else, and Caesar as consul was precisely what the Senate wished to avoid.

On the negative side Caesar lost a good officer when Labienus defected to the opposing side. He hailed from Picenum where Pompeian influence was strong and considered that he would be better off with Pompey; he may have been piqued because Antony's career was advancing faster and more spectacularly than his own. On the positive side, the roads to Rome were open, and Pompey evacuated the city, taking with him all who wished to accompany him, including the consuls and many magistrates. The government of Rome fled as Caesar advanced. From Pompey's point of view, it was the correct military decision, but it shocked his senatorial entourage. He sent a message to Lucius Domitius Ahenobarbus at Corfinium to follow him to Brundisium, but Domitius would not budge. He thought he could block Caesar's progress through Picenum, but Pompey knew that heroics were out of the question. It would be necessary to abandon not only Rome but also Italy to take his half-formed army somewhere else to train it and build up its strength. He left Domitius to his fate and made for Brundisium. At Corfinium, Caesar surrounded the town; Domitius' soldiers surrendered and Caesar took them into his own army, allowing all the officers and men of rank to go free, to join Pompey if they wished to. Caesar made much of this in his propaganda at the time, and when he wrote it up for the benefit of posterity he used the interviews he had with some of the men to put forward his own case for the defence, justifying his actions and throwing the blame for the war onto the Senate and the senatorial party who opposed him. He portrayed himself as the defender of the sacrosanctity of the tribunes and of the freedom of the Roman people from the oppression of a faction.

Pompey hurried to Brundisium to embark his troops, chased southwards by Caesar, who was anxious to prevent Pompey from leaving Italy. He marched at a merciless pace, sending messages to ask for talks and negotiation, but all to no avail. Pompey had gone too far now to back

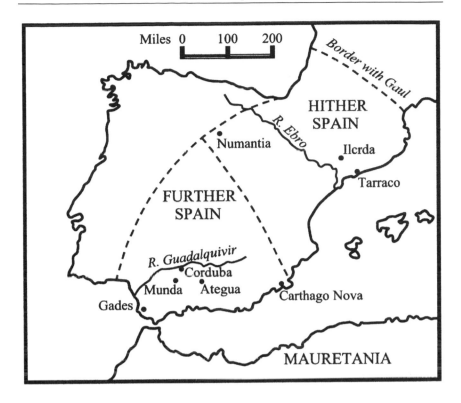

16 Map of Spain. The Spanish provinces were held by the Pompeians Lucius Afranius and Marcus Petreius and Varro. Caesar said that he was going to Spain to deal with the army without a leader, and then he would go to Greece to deal with the leader without an army. Drawn by Jan Shearsmith

down; whereas Caesar still had some mileage to make out of a public demonstration of his willingness, even eagerness, to settle the matter peacefully. But he was not given the chance to show how he could bring the war to an end. At Brundisium Pompey had dug trenches and fortifications across the approaches to the harbour, and behind these defences he shipped the first of his troops across the Adriatic to Greece, while the remainder waited for the transports to return. Then he embarked the last of the troops and sailed away. He now controlled two armies flanking Italy, one in Spain and the other in Greece, with Caesar in between.

Deprived of an immediate enemy to fight, Caesar returned to Rome, where he assembled the senators who were left, and tried to form a government. It was important to observe all the proper forms, so Caesar did not enter the city, because legally he could not cross the city boundary, the *pomerium*, while he was in command of troops. Under one heading he did not observe the proper forms at all. He seized all the money in the *aerarium*, the treasury. War was costly, and it was advisable to pay the soldiers. The prime purpose of the treasury, formed in the early Republic after Rome had been sacked by the Gauls, was to finance war against them should another invasion occur. There was a terrible curse on anyone who removed the money for other purposes, but as Caesar pointed out, he had conquered the Gauls, so he would be immune from the curse. He probably regarded the cash as payment in arrears for his services.

It was politic to honour his promises, so one of his first measures was to enfranchise the Cisalpine Gauls; the praetor Lucius Roscius attended to the necessary legislation. Before he embarked on the next military campaign, Caesar secured Italy and the provinces over which he had some control. Antony was left in charge of Italy, with Marcus Aemilius Lepidus as prefect of the city; Antony's brother Gaius was sent to Illyricum, Marcus Crassus, the son of the consul who died on the Parthian campaign, was put in command of Cisalpine Gaul, and Curio was sent to Sardinia and Sicily, with the eventual intention of going on to Africa.

Instead of following Pompey to Greece, Caesar chose Spain as his theatre of action. He said that he was going to deal with the army with no commander, then he would return to deal with the commander with no army. Since he had no ships, he had to approach Spain overland. He counted on the probability that Pompey was not yet ready to invade Italy, and there would be time to eliminate the Pompeians in the west before he had to deal with the Pompeians in the east. On the journey to Spain the route was blocked by the citizens of Massilia, who closed their gates against him. They had received notification from Pompey that Domitius Ahenobarbus was on his way to help them, and Caesar learned that Vibullius, one of the officers whom he had set free at Corfinium, was already there urging the Massiliotes to resist the Caesarians. Negotiations achieved nothing, and Caesar could not afford to waste too much time, so he left Gaius Trebonius in charge of three new legions to besiege the town, while he marched on into Spain.

Pompey's legates in Spain were Lucius Afranius, Marcus Petreius, and Varro. Between them they commanded seven legions. Afranius and Petreius had occupied Ilerda (modern Lerida) on the river Sicoris (the Segre) and placed their camp on a low hill south-west of the town; Caesar's general Fabius, sent on ahead from Gaul, had camped opposite them, perhaps to the north. He had built two bridges across the river to give his troops access to the lands to the east of it, and one of them had been destroyed in a storm. At this point Caesar arrived.

First of all he tried to isolate Afranius' camp from the town of Ilerda, where he had laid up all his supplies and stores. To achieve this he attempted to occupy some high ground between the enemy camp and the town, but he was thwarted because Afranius beat off the Fourteenth legion and then garrisoned the hill with his own troops. This reversal was followed by another, when Fabius' bridges collapsed. It was now impossible to forage east of the river, and the supply trains from Gaul could not reach Caesar until the bridges were rebuilt. Afranius attacked the supply convoy, but failed to press home the attack; at least it was not annihilated, a point which Fuller has questioned, because there was no reason why Afranius' victory should not have been total.

Without supplies and forage, Caesar now had to solve the problem of Ilerda or move off to find food. In order to cross the river, he made coracles, small boats made of wattle frames covered with hides, such as he had seen in use in Britain. He chose a point about a day's march upstream, and once enough men had been ferried across the river, he occupied and fortified some high ground. From there he was able to use the cavalry to good effect in harassing Afranius' foraging parties; many of the Pompeians were killed. The reversal of fortune perhaps influenced the Spanish towns; they had their hopes raised by a rumour that Pompey himself was marching through Africa to ship men across the Straits of Gibraltar to come to the aid of Afranius, but then when the rumour proved to be false, their hopes were dashed, and they began to think of allying with Caesar, since he seemed to be most likely to win the war, and ultimately it would be better to have been on the winning side all along. Several towns sent envoys to Caesar. Even better, some towns offered to supply his army.

Having gained the upper hand, Caesar embarked on an enormous task to create a man-made ford across the river, near the town. At one point there were three channels flowing round two islands, and at this part of the river Caesar decided to dig more channels to drain off more water and reduce the flow. Before he had managed to construct the artificial ford, Afranius and Petreius saw that he would be able to prevent them from gathering supplies from the lands lying east of the river, so their only course was to abandon Ilerda. They decided to aim for the river Ebro. In this area, the name of Pompey was well known, but Caesar would be seen as the hostile invader.

The Pompeians did not immediately move the whole army. As a preliminary they sent messages to the tribes living near the Ebro to construct a bridge at Octogesa, nearly 30 miles south of Ilerda, and also to collect boats. The delay in evacuating their camp meant that the Pompeians had allowed more time for Caesar to complete the ford. The river level dropped sufficiently to risk sending the cavalry across, but the infantry were endangered by the strength of the current, and in places the water was up to their armpits. The soldiers clamoured to make the attempt, however, especially as they saw Afranius and Petreius marching off, making rapidly for the high ground several miles away. Caesar's troops were close behind them, and the Pompeians flagged before they reached their objective, so they made camp, hoping to be able to slip away at dead of night. Caesar camped close by. He knew that there was a plan to build a bridge over the Ebro at Octogesa, and decided to make a rapid march with part of the army to get there first and block the approach to the river. He set off unencumbered with his baggage train, with the Pompeians marching almost as fast once they realised what he was about. It turned into a race; Caesar won. The Pompeians now had Caesarian troops behind them and in front of them, and lost many of their men when they tried to gain one of the highest hills. Caesar did not press home any further attacks, contrary to the wishes of his officers and men; he contented himself with making camp near the Pompeians, and preventing them from reaching the Ebro.

During the inaction, the troops began to fraternise. It seemed that Caesar would be able to negotiate and bring about a bloodless victory, until Petreius tightened discipline, and ordered the execution of any Caesarian soldiers found in his camp. Caesar's response was to send back unharmed the Pompeians found in his camp; he always had a strong instinct for effect, and knew very well that he would gain nothing by killing the men, but he would accrue very much more credit for letting them go free. It looked so much more civilised to contemporaries, and would enrich his fame and glory down the ages. And it cost nothing. Had there been a political advantage, he would have killed the soldiers on the spot.

Shortage of food, and more important, water, would force the Pompeian commanders to move sooner or later. A return to Ilerda was all they could think of, so they began a hazardous march with Caesar in pursuit. They camped on unsuitable ground, still without access to water, and tried to fortify themselves, while Caesar began to erect a counter fortification to enclose them. As a last resort, Afranius and Petreius drew up their army in battle order, but Caesar did not take the bait. He did not need to, knowing that time alone would decide the issue. The Pompeians knew it too, and surrendered.

Caesar stipulated that the enemy troops must be dispersed, and offered the soldiers supplies and a safe passage home. Of the Pompeians all that was left now was Varro in Further Spain; Quintus Cassius Longinus was despatched with two legions to watch him. Caesar summoned representatives from the towns to meet him at Corduba. They agreed to close their gates to Varro and deny him supplies, which gave Varro the choice of making his men fight on empty stomachs against an enemy who held most of Spain. He was loyal to Pompey, but he was also an educated man with common sense. He too surrendered. In order to secure Spain, Caesar left Cassius in command with four legions.

Returning to Massilia he caught up with the latest news. Trebonius was still besieging the town, and while Caesar was still in Spain, Decimus Brutus, with his naval expertise acquired in the battle against the Veneti, had smashed a Pompeian fleet. In Rome, Marcus Aemilius Lepidus had arranged Caesar's appointment as Dictator. The civil war affected most parts of the Roman world, and Caesar already controlled half of it. Even where there were no battlegrounds, or where the fighting had finished, he still had to expend troops to guard and garrison, Dolabella in command of ships, Cassius in Spain, Gaius Antonius in Illyricum, Curio in Africa; ultimately none of them did well. The Pompeian naval forces defeated Dolabella, offsetting the victory of Decimus Brutus; Cassius proved too arrogant in Spain and lost the goodwill of the people; when Gaius Antonius marched from Illyricum to counter the Pompeians he was defeated and surrendered. The worst disaster of all was Curio's defeat and death in Africa. It seemed that only in a few cases did Caesarians win when Caesar himself was not present; he must have subscribed heavily to the old adage that if you want to get anything done, do it yourself.

The successes in Spain did not impress all the troops. Those sent back to Italy were mutinous by the time Caesar arrived, over which particular grievance is not known, but it was probably because they had not received their promised rewards or had not found their opportunities for enrichment in Spain as profitable as they had expected. The Ninth legion seemed to be the most disaffected; Caesar proposed to decimate it, choosing every tenth man for execution. He perhaps used this threat as a deterrent, since after all he could not afford to lose so many men if he wished to carry the war to Greece; in the end he rounded up 120 of the most violent agitators and executed 12 of the ringleaders.

As Dictator Caesar could hold the consular elections; he himself was elected along with Publius Servilius Isauricus, the son of his old commander. The magistracies and the vacant priesthoods were all filled. Caesar was careful to act within the bounds of established custom, engaged in a frenzy of political activity before he went to make war on Pompey in Greece. His legislation was designed to relieve the burden of debt without upsetting the creditors, and to distribute food to the needy in Rome. He used his powers as Dictator to oil the wheels and hasten the necessary measures, achieving in a hectic eleven days as much as some magistrates would have taken the whole of their term of office to bring about. Caesar as Dictator, minus most of the Senate and the Pompeian magistrates, was able to avoid the debate that would normally have attended upon his measures, clause by clause. He may even have missed

Cato's voice, cleverly but routinely arguing against whatever it was that he proposed. He was in a hurry, eager to leave Italy to find Pompey, and decide the issue between them once and for all.

The army was assembling at Brundisium; some units were still on the march when Caesar arrived. He did not have enough transports to ferry the whole of his army across the Adriatic all at once, so he embarked 15,000 legionaries and 500 cavalry, encouraging them to leave their slaves and excess baggage behind so that he could carry more fighting personnel. The rest of the army was left behind at Brundisium in Antony's hands, ready to embark as soon as the transports returned. Everything was against Caesar, and it says much for his charisma as a leader that his troops trusted him and did not mutiny at the thought of what he was asking them to do, to cross the sea in winter with all the attendant dangers from storms and rough seas, to avoid the enemy fleet patrolling the eastern coast of Greece, to land in territory occupied by Pompey's troops, with only part of the army and the rest of it perhaps unable to join them for some time. The one point in his favour was that no one in the enemy camp expected Caesar to move so fast; they considered that he would not open a fresh campaign until spring.

The Pompeian fleet was commanded by Marcus Calpurnius Bibulus, Caesar's bitter enemy. He had no scouting vessels out when Caesar crossed the Adriatic unopposed, landing at Palaeste on the coast of Greece, about 50 miles north of the Pompeian naval base off Corcyra (modern Corfu). Bibulus soon learned that he had missed the opportunity to eliminate or disperse Caesar's transports, and put out to sea, catching 30 of the transports as they made the return journey to Italy to pick up Antony and the remaining troops. Bibulus' pent up frustration and anger of several years was vented on the crews of these ships; he burnt them to death along with the vessels. From now on Antony would have a difficult time trying to embark the rest of Caesar's army to ship them across the Adriatic, because the Pompeians watched Brundisium for the least movement, effectively blockading him in the port.

Though the time for negotiation was long past, Caesar nevertheless sent a message to Pompey, pointing out the uselessness of so many deaths if the two sides fought, and proposing that the Senate and the people of Rome should arrange the conditions for peace. In the ascendant politically because he controlled Rome, Caesar was in no position to dictate terms, or even to bargain. He was currently outnumbered, and uncertain as to when the rest of his troops would be able to join him. It was predictable that Pompey would refuse to accept the arbitration of the Senate, but the offer of negotiation portrayed Caesar as the one who was doing all he could to avoid war, and Pompey as the intransigent one who wanted war. Pompey knew exactly what was happening; the message was delivered by Vibullius Rufus, who had been captured by Caesar at Corfinium, released, and captured again in Spain. That alone demonstrated Caesar's *clementia*, his studied policy of mercy. After the first few words, Pompey stopped listening, growling that he did not wish to live the rest of his life by the grace of Caesar. The war was still on, and would have to be fought to the bitter end.

The coastal cities of Epirus surrendered to Caesar without a struggle, including Oricum and Apollonia. Pompey was marching at that very moment to occupy Apollonia and set up his base there, so when he heard that Caesar was already in possession of the city, he turned towards Dyrrachium instead, and a race began with the two armies, marching neck and neck for all they were worth to reach it first. Pompey won the race, not without casualties since his troops were not used to such punishing speeds on the march. Caesar withdrew, and made camp on the south side of the river Apsus, near Apollonia. Having established his headquarters and stores at Dyrrachium, Pompey camped on the north side of the river, but neither side offered battle. Pompey calculated that the lack of supplies would eventually force Caesar to move. The Pompeians could be supplied by sea and had a secure base at Dyrrachium, while Caesar had no choice but to keep on widening his foraging areas, going further and further afield as the country was stripped of produce. Caesar responded to this by occupying a strip of coastline opposite the Pompeian fleet base on the island of Corcyra, preventing them from landing to gather water and wood. It was a constant problem for the Pompeians to obtain fresh water, so this movement on the part of Caesar contributed to the harassment of the enemy fleet. Bibulus was a conscientious commander, who kept his ships at sea constantly to blockade Antony and patrol the Adriatic. He was ill, but would not stand down, and eventually died in post. Pompey did not appoint another overall senior commander of the fleet.

Another attempt to engage in meaningful dialogue was initiated by Caesar, and failed once again. His soldiers began to make encouraging speeches to the Pompeians across the river, but Labienus brought this fraternisation to a rousing end by shouting that there could never be peace until Caesar's head was delivered to Pompey. The source for these attempts to make peace is Caesar's own account of the civil war, which was probably written by Aulus Hirtius from his notes. It adds one more clause to the growing body of consistent and unrelenting Caesarian propaganda to spread the word that it was the Senate and the Pompeians who insisted upon war.

Waiting for Antony to bring the rest of the army from Italy, and growing increasingly impatient, Caesar famously tried to return to Italy in a small boat, wrapped in his cloak and anonymity, until the captain was

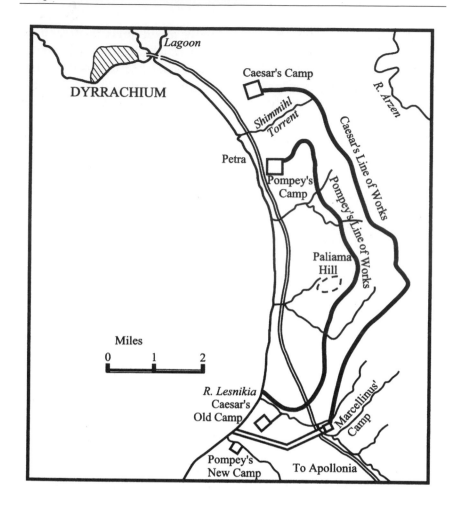

17 *Plan of the Dyrrachium campaign. Pompey held the town of Dyrrachium where he could receive supplies because he was supreme at sea. When Caesar started to invest his camp, Pompey extended his own lines to stretch Caesar's even further, and to extend his own foraging area within his lines. The campaign depended upon Pompey's efforts to break out, which he did eventually by attacking the southern end of Caesar's lines where he had not joined them up with a protective fortification.* Drawn by Jan Shearsmith

about to turn back, and then he tried to encourage the sailors by explaining that there was no need to fear; 'You carry Caesar and his fortune' he said, as though that granted immediate immunity from meteorological and oceanic threats. It patently did not, and he had to turn back, forced to rely on Antony to bring the troops to Greece. It is characteristic that Caesar thought that once he had arrived in Italy he would be able to find the answers to all the problems and set sail with his army. Locked up at Brundisium in enforced inactivity, Antony faced the Pompeian naval commander, Lucius Scibonius Libo, who occupied as his base the nearby island of Santa Andraea. As usual, the fleet lacked fresh water, so Antony placed a guard on all the places where the fleet might land to collect water, then sat back and waited. As soon as Libo withdrew, Antony embarked his troops; presumably they were constantly at the ready, awaiting the opportunity to sail. The winds were contrary, but that was less important than the fact that Libo's ships were not there to oppose Antony. He was blown off course, and missed his landing near Apollonia; instead he landed at Nymphaeum, north of Dyrrachium, got all the troops on shore and set off at once on the southward march to join Caesar. Pompey knew of the landing and tried to cut him off, but Antony evaded him, perhaps by good use of scouting parties, good luck, or a combination of both. Pompey lost no time in moving off when he realised he had lost the advantage of surprise, and was now sandwiched between two Caesarian armies, one to the north and one to the south.

When Antony joined up with Caesar, the army camped opposite Pompey near Asparagium in the valley of the Genusus (the modern river Skumbi), about a day's march from Dyrrachium. To remain there was impossible once the food supply ran out, so Caesar marched off. Pompey assumed he was going to find food, but was then informed that he had turned northwards, which could only mean that he was heading for Dyrrachium. A second race began. Caesar arrived first but his occupation of the area was nullified by the fact that Pompey seized the high ground of Petra, where he could still be supplied from the sea, so even though he could not move his whole army into Dyrrachium he was not at a disadvantage. Caesar began to build fortifications around Pompey's camp, enclosing it on three sides to prevent him from foraging over a wide area. Pompey rapidly extended his camp, erecting fortified lines to force Caesar to extend his own lines further and further to encompass them, stretching his resources of manpower. At one point in the proceedings, Pompey judged that Caesar was about to turn his fortifications from the north/south route towards the west, to meet the sea. He attacked suddenly, driving off the Caesarians commanded by Antony, then occupied the area himself, having considerably extended his foraging grounds in the process.

Caesar tried all the stratagems that he had used in Gaul, first cutting off part of the water supply to the Pompeians. The enemy dug wells but they quickly dried up, and in the end, because the horses were suffering, Pompey sent the cavalry by sea to Dyrrachium, where they could be fed and watered. A deserter came to Caesar offering to betray Dyrrachium

111

18 Mark Antony as an older and more experienced general. He was left in charge of the remaining troops at Brundisium after Caesar sailed with only half his army to follow Pompey. Antony successfully drew off the Pompeian fleet and brought the rest of the army to join Caesar, and played an important part in the main battles, including the final conflict at Pharsalus. Courtesy Musée Archéologique, Narbonne; photo Jean Lapage

and surrender the place to him. It was worth the attempt, because to seize it would be to deprive Pompey of his stores and naval base, so Caesar led out troops with the object of taking Dyrrachium. It soon became obvious that the deserter was a double agent who had led Caesar into a trap. The Pompeians attacked from the sea, and Caesar barely escaped with his life. Significantly, either because Caesar did not want to elaborate upon his near defeat, or because he could not take notice of what was happening and therefore did not have any meaningful or comprehensive notes, there is no full description of this battle in the account of the civil war.

Simultaneously with the attack on Caesar at Dyrrachium, the Pompeians attacked his camp at three different points. Publius Sulla had been left in command; he kept his head, repulsed one attack, and sent the German horsemen to deal with another. The Caesarians were extremely hard-pressed by Pompey's archers; after the battle the shield belonging to a centurion called Cassius Scaeva was brought to Caesar, displaying 120 arrow holes in it. Caesar went overboard in rewarding the soldiers who had been involved in this onslaught: 200,000 sesterces and promotion to

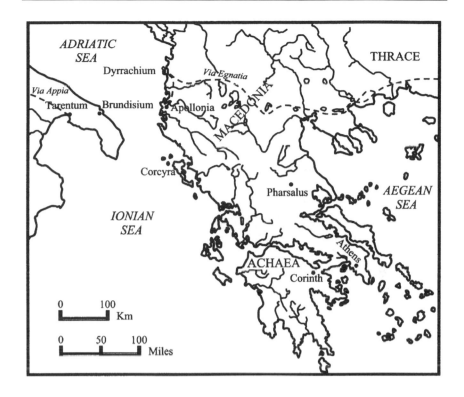

19 Map of Greece where Caesar and Pompey fought the battles of the civil war. The Pompeian fleet under Bibulus was based at Corcyra. Caesar evaded capture to land on the coast with only half his troops, and Antony eventually brought up the remaining troops, landing north of Dyrrachium, where Pompey eventually made camp and where Caesar blockaded him. Pompey broke the blockade, and the two armies marched to Pharsalus. The decisive battle there made Caesar the unchallenged victor, though the surviving Pompeians gathered in Africa while Caesar was in Egypt. Drawn by Jan Shearsmith after Graeme Stobbs

the high rank of *primus pilus* for Scaeva, and double pay, food and clothing for the soldiers.

For a short time after this attack, Pompey was able to push his lines forward to enclose more land, but soon had to withdraw to the original lines. Caesar made another attempt to negotiate, this time through Pompey's father-in-law, Metellus Scipio, who was in command of another Pompeian army, and had set out from Syria to join Pompey. This attempt at negotiation failed like all the others, defeated this time by one of Cato's circle, Marcus Favonius. Caesar was probably not surprised, and now concentrated on building two more camps near to Dyrrachium to prevent the Pompeian cavalry from foraging, with the result that

113

Pompey had to ship them all back to his camp so that they were once again enclosed within Caesar's lines, limited to the small foraging area and dependent on supplies from the sea. He was now back where he started, and could not remain bottled up for ever. It was time for Pompey to try to break out. He learned from two tribesmen of the Allobroges who deserted Caesar that the entrenchments that Caesar had dug were not completed at the southern end of the defences. There was a double line round the southern edge of Pompey's camp, one facing inwards to ward off attack from the Pompeians inside the camp, and one facing outwards in case troops came upon Caesar from the south. At the western end of the two lines, where they met the sea, they were still open, without the transverse fortification that Caesar intended to build to join them up, but had not yet completed. It would be possible to come in from the sea and get between the two lines, and also to land another party to attack the outer defences from the south. Pompey had already occupied a camp inside his own lines, facing the Caesarian northern defences. This would mean that Pompey would be able to surround the Caesarians, attacking from three sides at once. He put 60 cohorts into his camp facing Caesar's lines, then launched a sea-borne attack. He almost succeeded in driving off all the Caesarians. In the ensuing confusion when the guards at the open end of the double lines were driven back and started to run away inside the lines, they impeded the progress of the troops that the commander, Marcellinus, tried to send out to help them. It was Antony who retrieved the situation, arriving with fresh troops and holding off the attacks until Caesar arrived with 13 cohorts. The Pompeians were held off. Caesar lost some of his fortified lines, and started to repair them, and also tried to regain the camp that Pompey had occupied to the north of the Caesarian lines. At first he managed to drive the 60 cohorts out and install his own troops, but Pompey himself suddenly appeared with five legions. It was a rout, with many Caesarian losses. Pompey was hailed as Imperator by his troops. The implacable and bloodthirsty Labienus killed all the captives; it was a necessary measure because Pompey could not afford to feed them, but quite apart from necessity, Labienus enjoyed the slaughter.

A more important gain for Pompey was the camp he had been able to establish to the south of Caesar's lines, which enabled him to forage in the open country and feed his horses. The blockade had failed, and now Caesar would have to break camp and move into Thessaly. He sent one legion and the baggage to Apollonia, evacuating the lines in two stages. Pompey followed as soon as he realised that Caesar was marching away. The two armies eventually reoccupied their old camps near Asparagium in the Genusus valley. When Pompey set out to follow Caesar he had not brought with him all the baggage, so some of his men

20 *Plan of the Forum of Caesar, also called the Forum Julii, showing the Senate House at the southern end. Before the battle of Pharsalus, Caesar vowed that he would dedicate a temple to Venus Victrix if he won the battle and the campaign. When he did build it, the temple was dedicated to his mythical ancestress Venus Genetrix, and he set it within a huge Forum for*

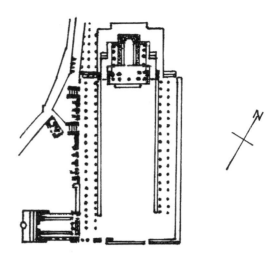

the use of the Roman people. The Senate House was burned down in 52 in the riots that followed the death of Clodius; the mob used it as Clodius' funeral pyre. Caesar undertook to rebuild it, and began the project in 44, but building stopped in the civil wars that followed his death. Augustus completed the work and dedicated it in August 29. Drawn by Jaqui Taylor

went back without orders to retrieve their belongings, weakening Pompey's army and spreading indiscipline, which Pompey was unable to quell. Caesar could see what was happening and chose this moment to break camp and march off, knowing that it would be some time before Pompey could assemble enough troops to follow him. There were many wounded in Caesar's army, so he lodged them at Apollonia, where he had already placed a legion, and he also garrisoned Oricum. In his account of the war, this is the point at which Caesar reviewed the possibilities of what might happen next. His fighting forces were reduced in numbers because of the many wounded and the garrisons he left behind. In addition two legions were detached from the main force under the command of Domitius Calvinus, sent to watch the army of Metellus Scipio. It was possible that Pompey would choose to go to the aid of his father-in-law and attack Domitius, in which case Caesar would have to follow and risk an open battle. Alternatively if Pompey took the opportunity to return to Italy, Caesar would not be able to sail after him because he had not enough ships, and would therefore have to march overland and invade from the north, just as he had done from Gaul, but this time the Pompeians would have had sufficient time to make better preparations. Another choice facing Pompey was to put

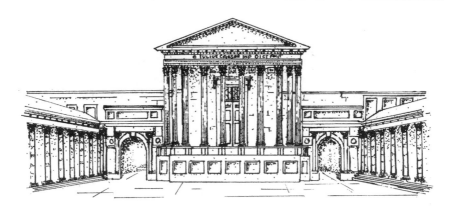

21 *Reconstruction of the Forum of Caesar showing the temple of Venus Genetrix.*
Drawn by Jacqui Taylor

Apollonia under siege, in which case Caesar would join Domitius and attack Metellus Scipio to draw Pompey off.

In the end Pompey yielded to criticism from his officers and the senators who were constantly at his heels advocating battle. He marched to join Scipio. Caesar sent messengers to warn Domitius, but they did not reach him, so he was unaware of Pompey's advance until it was almost too late, but he managed to get away by marching south to the valley of the Aliacmon (Vistritza). Either by accident or design, Caesar met him at Aeginium (modern Kelambaka). The united Caesarian armies turned south and made for Gomphi, about 20 miles away. Pompey had sent messages to all the towns in Thessaly that he had won a resounding victory at Dyrrachium, so the citizens of Gomphi assumed that Caesar was the loser, and was in retreat. They prudently closed their gates, in case by admitting Caesar they incurred the wrath of Pompey. It was a mistake, because Caesar stormed the town. His troops were allowed to sack it. Other towns in Thessaly revised their opinions and declared for Caesar.

The crops were ripening in Thessaly — it was August by the Roman calendar but early summer by the seasons — so Caesar chose a campsite near to the food supply. It was near to a place called Pharsalus, though Caesar does not name the place in his commentaries, and later sources cannot decide between Pharsalus itself and Old Pharsalus, two sites which lie about seven miles apart on the river Enipeus (Kutchuk Tcharnali). When Pompey arrived and camped nearby, Caesar offered battle every day without success, drawing up his troops closer and closer to the Pompeian camp. All to no avail. Pompey displayed his troops every day, but that was all, display and no substance. Pompey's strategy was to wear Caesar out, and he perhaps never knew how close he came to

22 Drawing of the Forum of Caesar as it appears today. Drawn by Jaqui Taylor

succeeding, because he succumbed to the constant nagging of his subordinates, who thought they could conduct the war much better than the commander and were so eager to see Caesar defeated that they could not wait for the long slow starvation process to take effect. Thus it was that on the very morning when Caesar had given the order to break camp and march away, he noticed that the Pompeians were beginning to draw up in front of their camp, but much further down the hill than usual. It was now or never. He halted the withdrawal and started to assemble for battle. Pompey's plan was to use his cavalry, superior in numbers, to attack Caesar's right wing, and then come in round the flank and rear of the Caesarians. Caesar drew up his army three lines deep, and noticing the build up of horsemen on the Pompeian left, he put Publius Sulla in command of his own right and remained there himself. He could not hope to sustain the attack with only 1000 cavalry of his own, so he withdrew some of his troops and placed them out of sight, to use as a

117

fourth line in addition to the normal three. The centre was commanded by Domitius Calvinus, and the left by Antony, with the Ninth legion, much reduced at Dyrrachium, and the Eighth legion, brigaded together.

The battle opened with a charge from Caesar's side. Pompey stood his ground to receive the charge, because he did not wish his troops to be winded by the time they started to fight. When battle was joined, Labienus took the cavalry and charged Caesar's right wing. They failed to envelop the wing entirely and were panicked by the sudden appearance of the troops that Caesar had drawn off and concealed. They took the Pompeians in flank and scattered them. This was the turning point, and combined with the simple but unorthodox fighting methods that Caesar had advocated, that of striking at the faces of the Pompeians, the battle became a rout. When Labienus' cavalry had been driven off, the Pompeian left wing was unprotected, and Caesar's fourth line pressed home. At the same time he sent in the third line to help the first and second on the whole front.

Pompey's troops turned and fled back to camp, and Pompey himself left the field, knowing that there was nothing more that he could do. The Caesarians pursued, right through the camp, where discipline and the main object of the battle were preserved, because they did not stop to plunder, and went on chasing the fugitives. The remnants of the Pompeian army reached some high ground and stayed there all night, but they surrendered next day, because they were without a commander, and Caesar cut off the water supply to their makeshift camp. Caesar toured the battlefield, and surveying the dead, according to Suetonius, he expressed his regrets and threw the blame on the Senate and Pompey with the phrase 'They would have it so. I, Julius Caesar, would have been condemned if I had not appealed to the army for help.'

The battle was won but the war was not yet over. The figurehead was not accounted for among the casualties, and there were other Pompeians still at large. The fleet alone was a major force to be reckoned with. If Caesar left the east to go to Rome, the Pompeians could reassemble and gain strength; respect for the name of Pompey was not yet extinguished among the independent and client kingdoms. It would be better to neutralise or remove the figurehead, Pompey himself, and then deal with recalcitrant opposition piecemeal, section by section. Then Caesar would see how the land lay in Italy. He had to take the chance that his adherents in Italy and the provinces would prove strong and hold out against the Pompeians. To this end he despatched Antony to Rome, and Domitius Calvinus to govern Asia with three legions recruited from the Pompeian troops. But where was Pompey? News came that he had gone to Cyprus. Caesar knew where he would aim for next. He would have to follow Pompey to Egypt.

7 Alexandria, Thapsus, and Munda

Pompey's arrival in Egypt was not greeted with unalloyed pleasure. There was a private war going on between the young Ptolemy XIII and his half-sister Cleopatra VII, both of whom were declared the joint heirs of the deceased Ptolemy XII Auletes according to the terms of his will. Neither of them wished to share power with the other, and both of them had an entourage and an army with which to fight it out. Cleopatra had been driven out of Alexandria, and was with her army somewhere near the city. Ptolemy XIII was still only a boy, so his ministers dealt with most matters, including the arrival of Pompey. The three principal courtiers were Achillas, commander of the Royal army, Pothinus, the finance minister, and Theodotus, Ptolemy's tutor. There were several dangers that could arise from Pompey's presence in Egypt, besides the fact that hot on the heels of the defeated Roman general the victorious one might follow, bringing Roman war to Egyptian soil. The other possibilities were just as daunting. There were many Roman soldiers in the Royal army, who had been brought there by Pompey's general Aulus Gabinius when Ptolemy Auletes required support for his throne. Pompey could call on these men and they would perhaps rally to his call, weakening the Royal army and giving the advantage to Cleopatra. Worse still Pompey could choose to make overtures to Cleopatra and descend on Alexandria. There were several variations on this theme, and rather than risk facing any of them the courtiers of Ptolemy XIII decided to eliminate Pompey. 'Dead men don't bite', said Achillas.

Caesar's emotions can only be surmised when he arrived in Alexandria and was presented with Pompey's head and signet ring. Plutarch says that he shed tears; perhaps he did. Pompey had been married to his daughter Julia and had loved her dearly, and he had been a colleague for a long time. Caesar may have hoped that if he caught up with him soon enough he may have been able to talk to him, persuade him to work with him in Rome, and do great things together. Whatever he had planned it was now impossible. Pompey was converted into a martyr. His followers would probably stiffen their resolve, fight longer and harder, and continue the war in several quarters of the Roman world, whereas if Pompey could have been won over, the rest of the factions would perhaps have ended the war.

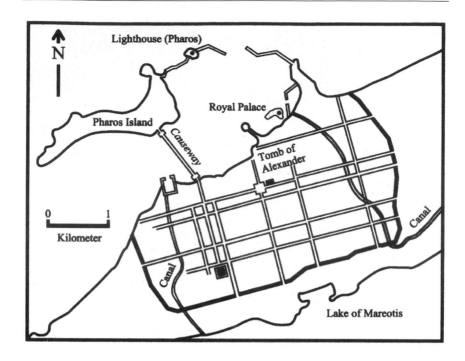

23 Plan of Alexandria. When Caesar arrived there in pursuit of Pompey, the city was held by Ptolemy XIII, and Cleopatra was with her army, preparing to fight a civil war with her half-brother. According to legend, she arrived at Caesar's feet in a rolled up carpet, and together they withstood a siege and emerged victorious when Caesar's relieving army arrived, under his ally Mithridates of Pergamum. Drawn by Jan Shearsmith after Graeme Stobbs

Once he was established in Alexandria with very few troops, Caesar allowed himself to become embroiled, perhaps deliberately, in the internal was between Ptolemy and Cleopatra. There was potential profit in remaining there. In his early career Caesar had entertained hopes of going to Egypt to arrange for its annexation, when Crassus interpreted the last will and testament of Ptolemy XI Alexander as a bequest of his kingdom to Rome. That scheme had come to nothing, but now there were four surviving children of Ptolemy XII Auletes, two of whom had been named as his heirs. The other children were a young boy also called Ptolemy, and a daughter of Auletes called Arsinoe. It would be worthwhile attempting to arbitrate, and pacify the situation so that the established rulers would be grateful to Rome, specifically to Julius Caesar.

Cleopatra's entry into history traditionally begins when she rolled out of a carpet at Caesar's feet. The legend may be true. When Caesar arrived,

24 Head of
   Cleopatra. This is
   one of the finest
   portrayals of the
   Queen of Egypt,
   and whilst it does
   not flatter her it
   bears a close
   relationship to the
   portraits of
   Alexander the
   Great. The severe
   hairstyle is
   reflected on
   Cleopatra's coin
   portraits.
   Courtesy
   Berlin Museen

Cleopatra was unable to march into Alexandria at the head of her army,
and did not dare to try to walk in openly because if she fell into the hands
of Achillas or Pothinus she would not have survived the experience.
Caesar was the most powerful general in the world at that time, and she
had to reach him quickly but secretly, banking on being able to persuade
him to take up her cause. The rolled up carpet carried by a faithful
servant is as good as any other tale as to how she arrived. Her association
with Caesar has overtones of sex and scheming; even respected modern
historians label her demonic, as though she cast some sort of spell over
Caesar, who then went on to set her up as Queen of Egypt because he
could not help himself. This is Augustan propaganda, casting Cleopatra
in the role of evil temptress who brought Antony to ruin and represented
the most fearsome threat to Rome since Hannibal. In reality, Caesar
probably reviewed the available material, the young Ptolemy XIII, the
even younger sibling Ptolemy, Arsinoe and Cleopatra, and then judged
Cleopatra to be the most sensible, knowledgeable, conscientious,
independent, and resourceful of the four; in a word, the most fit to rule.
When the Alexandrian war was over, she became Queen of Egypt with
Caesar's backing. To achieve this, Caesar had to endure a siege from an

25 *This relief from the temple at Dendera shows Cleopatra as the goddess Isis.* Photo David Brearley

unaccustomed angle; that is, from the inside. Achillas brought up Ptolemy XIII's army and invested the Royal palace with all four heirs to the throne inside it.

Caesar had already sent for reinforcements to be brought in by sea, and had contacted his ally Mithridates of Pergamum, sending him to Syria and Cilicia to recruit more troops, but he would have to wait for some time before these reinforcements reached him. His first concern was to eliminate the Egyptian fleet, so that his own ships could enter the harbour when they arrived with the troops. He burnt the Egyptian ships and, famously, the library as well. Immediately afterwards without a pause he seized the lighthouse, the Pharos, at the harbour mouth. As the days went by he concentrated on fortifying the Royal palace. Arsinoe fled to join Achillas and the army, taking her courtiers and entourage with her, one of whom called Ganymede soon quarrelled with Achillas, who was assassinated. Ganymede took over command of the army, applying himself to spoiling the fresh water supply of the palace by digging trenches to let sea water in. The Romans dug wells, and survived, but they could not do so indefinitely.

The next battle was for possession of the causeway on the western side of the harbour linking the Pharos with the mainland. While he was fortifying it Caesar's men were attacked, and many were drowned. Caesar himself had to leap into the sea and swim to shore, according to legend holding papers above his head to keep them dry. This reversal did not affect the situation too badly, because it was already dire enough if Caesar received no outside assistance. Fortunately the reinforcements were on their way. Just before Mithridates marched in from Syria, Ptolemy XIII was allowed to join the army besieging the Royal palace, and when Mithridates took Pelusium, east of Alexandria, he led the army out against him. Caesar followed and trapped and annihilated the Egyptians between two forces. Ptolemy was drowned in the Nile. According to Egyptian lore this conferred divinity upon him; Caesar had him fished out and put on display to demonstrate that he was mortal and dead.

Cleopatra was made Queen of Egypt with her young brother Ptolemy XIV as consort. Her true consort for the time being was Caesar himself. There were rumours that he had married her according to Egyptian rites; he could not legally marry her for two reasons: he was already married to Calpurnia, and in Roman law it was illegal for a Roman to marry a foreigner. Whether or not he went through any form of ceremony with her, their association must have begun very soon after her arrival in the palace; nine months later, after Caesar had departed, she gave birth to a son whom she called Ptolemy Caesar, and whom the Alexandrians nicknamed Caesarion, son of Caesar, or little Caesar. The child's parentage was not in doubt. He combined Egypt and Rome in his lineage. He represented the compromise between independence for Egypt and total absorption and annexation by Rome. The first was not really feasible without the support or good will of Rome, but the second was what Cleopatra most wanted to avoid.

Despite the turmoil in the rest of the Roman world, where the Pompeians were gathering strength at sea, in Africa, and even in Spain once again, Caesar remained in Egypt until the summer of 47. He would

26 *Cleopatra and Caesarion on the temple at Dendera in Upper Egypt. From the very first moment Cleopatra promoted Caesarion as her heir and successor, and made no secret of his parentage. Though Caesarion was unequivocally the son of a Roman, Cleopatra was concerned to place him firmly in an Egyptian context. On this and other monuments she depicted him as Horus to her Isis, in the costume and regalia of the Pharaohs. Combining Roman and Egyptian heritage, Caesarion represented the greatest threat to Caesar's testamentary heir and successor, Octavian, who had him killed after the deaths of Antony and Cleopatra and the fall of Alexandria in 30.* Photo David Brearley

not have been completely inert, but nothing has survived to attest to his activities, except that when he began to attend to the problems that had broken out in the eastern provinces he did not have to exert himself in prolonged preparation, nor did he have to fight to re-establish his position in Rome when he finally returned. His lieutenants and agents in all parts of the Roman world will have worked on his behalf, and though it seems that he did not communicate directly with Rome for the duration of his stay in Alexandria, it does not necessarily mean that he neglected to communicate with his armies elsewhere, or failed to keep himself informed of what was happening. In the autumn of 48, the Caesarians in Italy had procured his appointment as Dictator for one year (the normal term was for six months), and Mark Antony was made *magister equitum*, master of horse. He was Caesar's deputy in military and political matters, but not unrivalled. He faced trouble from Marcus Caelius Rufus, who joined forces with the exiled Titus Annius Milo, both of them men with grudges. Their joint programme centred on the debt-ridden masses of Rome. Eventually they both perished, but the cause of the debtors was taken up by Cornelius Dolabella. The watchword became cancellation of all debts, and there was a riot in the Forum. The Senate authorised Antony to restore order, and he did so, bloodily. He brought up his troops but the crowd did not disperse; he could not back down, and the mob would not back down; the troops went in and there were several deaths. When Caesar at last returned to Rome, Antony was coolly dropped, mostly because Caesar could not be seen to condone Antony's actions.

Before he left Egypt, Caesar did allow himself a short holiday; he and Cleopatra sailed up the Nile, advertising their union. It was a pleasure cruise mixed with business and politics. Cleopatra had more to gain than Caesar, but perhaps he also enjoyed the leisure it afforded him. He had been hyperactive for many years, balancing wars of conquest with constant political alertness; he was 53 years old going on 54, and still had some distance to go before he even began to achieve what he wanted in Rome. He could hardly be blamed if he took time to enjoy a cruise with a fascinating, clever, attractive if not beautiful young woman of 22.

He departed from Egypt, perhaps in June, concerned to quell the Empire-building activities of Pharnaces, the son of Mithridates whom Pompey had defeated. Already the Roman territories of Bithynia and Pontus were threatened. Pharnaces defeated Domitius Calvinus, and went on to take Amisus and Sinope, then occupied Pontus and set up his new kingdom there. The east was important to Rome, the whole area being balanced between independent kingdoms, allied kingdoms, and Roman provinces. This balance was easily upset, with knock-on effects resounding through all the territories. Pompey had made sensible and sensitive arrangements after his defeat of the elder Mithridates.

Caesar spent some time at Antioch in Syria and at Tarsus in Cilicia giving judgement in court cases and receiving footloose Pompeians who surrendered to him. Then he set out across Cappadocia and collected troops from Deiotarus, king of Galatia. This was by way of an indemnity payment from Deiotarus, who had backed the losing side and supported Pompey. Pharnaces was at Zela in Pontus, encamped near to the town and in occupation of the heights nearby. He counted on the turmoil in the rest of the Roman world to distract Caesar and force him to withdraw, so he negotiated, drawing out the proceedings in the hope that Caesar would eventually be compromised and perhaps agree to terms. But Caesar was not willing to be drawn into this game. Operations focused on the possession of high ground some distance from Caesar's camp. It was close to Pharnaces' camp but separated from it by a deep gully and well protected by the steep slope to the summit. Fully prepared with all the materials to build ramparts, the Caesarian troops marched out under cover of night somewhat encumbered by their tools and equipment, but once they were on the hilltop they were able to erect fortifications very quickly. Incredibly, Pharnaces launched a frontal attack on this camp, sending his troops across the ravine and up the steep side of the hill. At first Caesar did not believe his eyes and dismissed the attack as a display of bravado, smoke without fire, but then he realised that Pharnaces was deadly serious, so he had to organise his available troops very swiftly to meet the threat. The soldiers were not formed up in line of battle and might have been overwhelmed had not the Sixth legion managed to force the enemy back down the hill. The battle turned into a rout. The Romans chased Pharnaces and his troops all the way down the hill, up the opposite one and into their camp. But they did not capture Pharnaces.

The victory signalled the rapid departure of Caesar for Italy as soon as he had made the final administrative and military arrangements for the eastern provinces. He left two legions in Pontus to guard against any more attempts by Pharnaces to occupy it. He did not write the account of the war himself, but presumably he made rough notes of the main events which could be used by the real author of the work. But Caesar did write the famous phrase summing up his achievement, with its emphasis on the lightning campaign and its total success: '*veni, vidi, vici*' as he expressed it to his friend Gaius Matius, 'I came, I saw, I conquered'. Caesar was so pleased with the phrase that he used the slogan again in his triumph. In modern times Caesar could have run an advertising agency; in his own time what he advertised best was himself.

It was high time to return to Rome. He arrived in the autumn of 47, that is, autumn by the calendar, which was out of date; by the actual seasons it was mid-summer. He found Antony and Dolabella at loggerheads and a mounting problem over debts, which he did his best to alleviate. He held the consular elections in which his officers Fufius Calenus and Publius Vatinius received their rewards and were appointed consuls, for what short time remained of the year. In addition Caesar promoted and rewarded numbers of equites and senators. He promoted his great-nephew Gaius Octavius, now aged about sixteen, by appointing him *praefectus urbi* (city prefect) during the festival of the *Feriae Latinae*. This was an honorary post with little relevance to the duties that the later city prefects undertook, and it was often bestowed on young members of upper class families at the time of the festival, when all the magistrates left Rome in the hands of the priests, to travel to the Alban Mount to conduct religious ceremonies in memory of Roman conquest of Alba Longa. Gaius Octavius was therefore at the head of the state for two or three days, in charge of all administration of the city. Perhaps only a few people took serious note of him. He was very young and always ill with one complaint or another; on the face of it, nothing much could be expected of him.

From the political quarter Caesar experienced little trouble. He was Dictator for the second time, and after the continual disturbances of the last few years most people were content to allow him to organise as he wished. Apart from the powers that the Dictatorship bestowed on him, there was also the useful device of tribunician sacrosanctity contained within it. If contentment was among Caesar's attributes, he ought to have come close to it now.

The soldiers were not so happy. They were tired and wanted rest and the pay that had been promised them. There was soon to be a campaign in Africa against the Pompeians who were entrenched there, so this was the moment to make a stand, at the point where their commander would need them. They came to Rome and camped outside the city, where Caesar met them to listen to their demands. He was unprotected, though prudently he had ensured that Antony was close by with troops he could trust. He asked the soldiers what they wanted. They tried to bluff, saying that they wanted to be discharged, calculating that Caesar would consider their services indispensable, and would therefore try to persuade them to stay with him for the next campaign by making them offers that they could not refuse. Caesar knew his men and had no need of a psychology textbook or attendance on a management course. He addressed the soldiers as *Quirites*, citizens, and not as soldiers, as though their discharge was already a fact. He was gambling, just as the soldiers had gambled and lost, but he had the edge and the power, and he did it better than they did.

He added that he would indeed give them all that he had promised, once he had returned laden with booty from the wars in Africa, wars which he would fight using other troops, since they were not willing to go with him. No one questioned this; after all, Caesar found troop raising so easy, and he was never a blusterer, all words and no action; he probably *would* set off without the whole army. Besides, if they stayed in Italy there would be no chance of further pay and profit from the wars. The soldiers were soon eating out of Caesar's hand, begging to be taken to Africa.

Part of the army sailed from Lilybaeum in Sicily just as the winter season was beginning. Not unexpectedly, a storm blew up and scattered the ships; there was seemingly no pre-arranged rendezvous, because Caesar was not fully informed as to which harbours and coastal towns were in Pompeian hands and which were free. Consequently Caesar landed with no more than 3000 men and 150 cavalry, near Hadrumetum (modern Susa). He converted a potentially bad omen into a good one by presence of mind and thinking on his feet, or rather his knees; as he disembarked he fell, but came up again with handfuls of sand and earth, proclaiming 'I hold you, Africa'. Other generals in other places and at other times have used the same ploy. Soldiers need confidence in their commanders.

Hadrumetum was held by the Pompeian general Considius Longus, and Caesar did not attempt to take it. After a short rest, he marched south-east down the coast towards Leptis Minor (modern Lemta). The towns on the route welcomed him, including Leptis, and an additional stroke of luck was that some of the transports arrived at Leptis. But Caesar still did not have an adequate campaign army, and some of the ships were still unaccounted for. He sent the transports back to Sicily to bring over the rest of the troops, and put Vatinius in command of warships to look for the lost fleet.

While Caesar was in Egypt and the east, the Pompeians in Africa had used the interval to build up their strength. They had congregated at Utica where the governor Atius Varus was replaced by Cato. Juba, the king of the Numidians, joined them, bringing in valuable and experienced horsemen and archers as well as infantry. The citizens of Utica favoured Caesar, and Metellus Scipio advocated their massacre and the destruction of the city. It was Cato who successfully protested against this barbarous suggestion. He emerged as the true political leader, advocating a policy of wearing Caesar down by preventing him from foraging and keeping him away from the harbours and ports. But it was Metellus Scipio who was chosen as overall commander. Cato's supreme ability was overshadowed by his uncompromising nobility. He acquiesced in the choice of Scipio as commander because he had more experience and greater seniority; if Cato had taken command himself, the outcome of the war would perhaps have been very different.

After only a few days the transports that had been blown off course delivered the troops to Caesar, who made camp at Ruspina, a plateau north of Leptis Minor. Immediately he led out a forage party, flanked by archers for protection, but they ran into Labienus with his Gallic and German horsemen. After fighting their way almost back to camp, Caesar's men were attacked by Petreius, and started to panic. At one point Caesar had to seize a standard bearer who was running away, and manhandle him back into line, pointing out that the enemy soldiers were in fact situated in the opposite direction. Eventually Caesar and the surviving men broke through to higher ground, where they remained for a few hours, until he led them all back to camp in the dark. The historian Appian says that the Pompeians withdrew because Scipio was coming up with more troops and they wished to give him the opportunity of delivering the final blow. The whole episode is suspicious, and suffers from a lack of clear information in Caesar's description of the battle. There was no reason why he should not have been wiped out, attacked on two sides simultaneously or in succession, and it is strange that the Pompeians did not try to invest the high ground where Caesar took refuge, in order to prevent him from leaving and returning to camp.

After this battle Caesar's main concern was to find food. The Pompeians, united under the command of Scipio, camped near Ruspina, with the result that foraging became a hazardous enterprise for Caesar's men. He built two lines of entrenchments from Ruspina to the sea so that he could bring in supplies from his ships, and also more troops. He badly needed reinforcements, the more so since the towns nearby who needed his protection could so easily turn against him and declare for the Pompeians if he failed to send troops to aid them. Fortunately for the Caesarians, king Juba left Scipio to go home to attend to a rebellion that had begun while he was absent, fostered by Caesar and his allies, king Bocchus of Mauretania, and a Roman called Publius Sittius who resided in Bocchus' kingdom. They took Cirta (modern Constantine), the wealthiest city of Numidia, forcing Juba to fight his own battles instead of acting for the Pompeian cause.

The much-needed reinforcement for Caesar arrived at the end of January 46, comprising the Thirteenth and Fourteenth legions and some cavalry and archers. With his enlarged army he moved south to Uzita and made two camps, one on the high ridge to the east of the town and another nearer to Uzita itself. The usual skirmishes occurred when the soldiers were foraging, but Caesar was prepared; his troops clashed with Scipio's troops and Labienus, emerging the victors when Caesar introduced his extra cavalry that he had hidden behind some farm

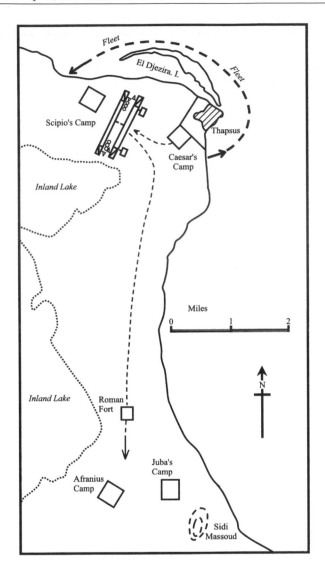

27 *The campaign of Thapsus. In order to tempt the Pompeians to give battle Caesar made camp near Thapsus in a seemingly disadvantageous position, between a marshy lake and the coast. The Pompeians set about blocking the landward escape routes while Caesar besieged the town of Thapsus from the landward side, also blockading it from the seaward approaches by means of his fleet. Instead of being held in a vice, Caesar managed to defeat Scipio, sandwiching him and his troops between his own army and some squadrons of ships, which sailed round to the rear of the Pompeians as though they were about to make a landing. It was the end of the war in Africa, and the surviving Pompeians went to Spain.* Drawn by Jan Shearsmith

buildings. There were no serious actions after this battle. Caesar tried to seize some high ground but Labienus reached it first, so having been foiled in the attempt, Caesar turned his attention to the town of Uzita, deciding to besiege it. Between the camp and the siege works there was a plain, so to protect the soldiers he built two parallel lines of defence. If he could take the town he could rely on its supplies for a while, but the siege failed, and lack of food forced him to move away.

More reinforcements from Sicily were due to arrive soon, so to enable them to land he detailed ships from the fleet at Leptis to guard the approaches to Hadrumetum, and also Thapsus on an eastward facing promontory further along the coast. The Pompeian admiral Varus set out from Utica with a large squadron to intercept the transports, and to destroy the rest of Caesar's ships at Leptis. As soon as Caesar was informed of the danger to the fleet, he mounted his horse and rode straight for Leptis, put out to sea in a small boat, located one of his detached squadrons watching the coastal towns, leapt on board one of the ships to take command, and returned to drive away Varus and the Pompeian fleet. He saved most of his ships from destruction and cleared the way for the Sicilian transports, which arrived shortly afterwards carrying the Ninth and Tenth legions. He took them to Uzita where the whole army was assembled, but he knew that he could not remain there, and soon abandoned the siege. He marched off towards Thapsus, and made camp about 15 miles from the town, with the Pompeians close behind him. Scipio camped to the west of Caesar's camp, and started to forage around the town of Zeta. In order to take the town of Zeta, Caesar had to march past the enemy camp, but he decided to attempt it. He occupied Zeta and installed a garrison, then on the return journey he was attacked by Labienus and Afranius, with the Numidian cavalry riding in and out, never fully engaging in battle. They could attack from all sides, encircling the Caesarians, without receiving any damage in return, then draw off very quickly, just as quickly regrouping for the next onslaught. The temptation when harassed like this was to make camp, but that would have been suicidal. There were no supplies, and more important no water, so to entrench themselves would be to condemn the Caesarians to a slow death while the Pompeians watched and waited. Caesar was having none of this and doggedly kept on moving, extremely slowly, beating off attacks as the troops plodded onwards. Discipline held, under tremendously exacting circumstances. The soldiers finally got back to camp at night. The experience decided Caesar to meet like with like; he began to train some of his soldiers, 300 men from each legion, to fight in loose formation instead of in the usual solid battle lines. This involved teaching them to fight as individuals, more like gladiators. He used the new formations against Labienus

28 Coin of Caesar Imperator. Caesar's was the first portrait that had appeared on a Roman coin. Before this time, only the heads of gods were depicted, though in the east, portraits of individual rulers were the norm on the coinage. In this respect it seemed that Caesar wished to emulate the eastern kings, perhaps in more ways than one. By placing his own portrait on the coinage it seemed that Caesar had taken the first step towards monarchy. Drawn by Jaqui Taylor

when the latter attacked him on the way to seize one of Scipio's stores bases at Sarsura.

So far Scipio had adhered to the policy of refusing to engage in pitched battles. Caesar's problem was how to make him change this policy, otherwise the war could drag on forever, and the longer it went on the more worn down his troops would become. He required a battlefield where it would seem that he and his troops were at a grave disadvantage, and where the Numidian cavalry could not operate, but where the legions could engage each other. He found it at Thapsus. The town was garrisoned by Pompeian troops under Gaius Vergilius. The main feature of the site, an advantage from the Pompeian point of view, was that in the hinterland there was only a narrow strip of land running north to south between the sea and an inland lake, so that if both ends of this corridor were blocked the army camped near to Thapsus would be boxed in. Caesar's fleet was already guarding the approaches to Thapsus from the sea, so now he began to besiege it from the land. He built a fort at the southern end of the land corridor between the coast and the lake, and made his main camp near the town and the siege works.

At first the Pompeians camped at the southern end of the corridor, but Caesar's camp hampered their movements. Leaving Juba and Afranius in situ, Scipio took part of the army and marched around the lake to erect a camp at the northern end, west of the town. Caesar was ready for this. He attacked, having given orders to the fleet blockading Thapsus to sail round the promontory to the rear of Scipio's army, to create confusion and perhaps make the Pompeians imagine that they were going to disembark troops. Scipio met the challenge by drawing up in battle formation with elephants on both wings. As at Pharsalus Caesar formed up extra troops out of sight, but this time he did so on both wings to deal with the elephants. Scipio's troops for some reason started to mill about in confusion, and the Caesarians, noticing the turmoil, urged Caesar to give the order to engage. He declined, but the soldiers were so eager to join battle that they could not be held back. Without any orders they charged. On Scipio's right the elephants panicked and ran away through the ranks of the Pompeian troops, causing mayhem as they went. The Numidian horsemen were infected with the panic, and they too left the field. The whole Pompeian army collapsed. Juba and Afranius abandoned their camps, but many of the soldiers fell victim to the pursuing Caesarians.

Scipio's surviving soldiers fled to Utica, where they disgraced themselves by killing many of the inhabitants when they forced their way into the town. Cato stopped the massacre, but he had to resort to bribery to persuade the men to leave the town. It was the end of the war in Africa. Pompeian resistance was confined to two towns, Thapsus and Thysdra, and then there was the fleet and the pockets of Pompeians and sympathisers in Spain. Cato could do nothing to stop Caesar from sweeping all before him, and he did not wish to flee to join the Spanish or naval contingents. He made the necessary arrangements for the welfare of his family, and committed suicide. It was the preferred option to being forgiven by Caesar.

One by one the other Pompeians were hunted down. Afranius was captured and Caesar executed him. Scipio was drowned trying to escape by sea. Juba and Petreius failed to find sanctuary, fought each other to the death, and the winner of the combat was killed by a slave. Shortly after the battle of Thapsus, the town surrendered, as did Thysdra. Caesar occupied Utica, Hadrumetum and Uzita, and took over the kingdom of Juba, some of which he handed over to Bocchus of Mauretania for his part in distracting Juba from the Pompeians. The majority of the kingdom was incorporated into the province of Africa, as the new province Africa Nova, with its first governor the proconsul Gaius Sallustius Crispus. The Roman officers who had served with Juba had their property confiscated, and fines were imposed on communities which had supported the Pompeians. Caesar settled some of his veterans in colonies in towns along the coast. It served the purpose of guarding the coast against the Pompeian fleet and partially solved the problem of veteran settlement when he returned to Rome. He had been absent for two years.

The Republic was in tatters and in dire need of restoration. There was hope that the Dictator would set things in order on the old pattern. Cicero was full of anticipation that he would do so, dropping strong hints and writing essays on how it should be done. But there was a potential conflict of interest, centred on perceptions of Rome and the Republic, and what it meant to various people. Caesar allegedly said that the *res publica* was just a name, which sentiment was taken to mean that he had no respect for it. The difference was one of scope; Romans thought of Rome at the centre of the universe, with satellites all around for exploitation and profit making. Caesar's ideas of Rome encompassed the wider world; he thought in Imperial terms. For that he needed to be Emperor, a position for which the Republic had no place.

The office of Dictator, which he still held, was originally intended to bestow on the holder the power to put into operation short-term emergency measures in time of crisis. When the crisis was averted or remedied, the office holder stepped down. It was the highest office in the Roman world and Caesar had no intention of letting go of it. His power was absolute, and honours mingled with yet more powers flowed in his direction. The most gratifying practical development was that the Dictatorship was renewed for ten years. In addition Caesar could sit between the consuls and speak first in debates, which gave him a preponderant influence, as if he needed any further influence beyond being Dictator. For his victories in Africa, an unprecedented 40 days' thanksgiving had been decreed by the Senate, and a triumphal chariot bearing a statue of him was placed inside the Capitoline temple. At the foot of the statue was a globe, proclaiming his divinity. The text of the inscription is not known, nor even the language; it may have been in Greek, but was more likely to have been in Latin, declaring him *divus*. The statue and its inscription offended people, so Caesar soon had the words removed. There is scholarly debate about what it all meant, and whether Caesar really intended to set himself up as a living god, and indeed whether he was aiming at the sort of divine monarchy that had firm roots in the east. If so, at this juncture he had to back down, contenting himself with the Dictatorship and the office of *praefectus morum*, prefect of morals, which derived from the censorship, and potentially gave him the opportunity to mark out and remove from their posts the men who did not measure up to the strict Roman behavioural code.

There was some dismay when Caesar did not demurely decline all the honours that were voted to him, though it can be inferred that he may have refused some that have not been recorded, since Dio says that he includes in his narrative only those honours that Caesar accepted, as though there were many more. Perhaps Caesar rejected the honours that carried no practical weight. He declared that he disapproved of despotism and would never emulate Sulla, Marius or Cinna — an attempt to come to terms with the past, perhaps, since the last two of this infamous trio were his own relatives. Reconciliation was the order of the day, but it did not please everyone, for a variety of reasons. Some of his own circle would have preferred to exterminate the Pompeians root and branch, while his opponents, like Pompey and Cato, indignantly questioned his authority to implement his famous policy of *clementia*, and did not wish to live literally at Caesar's mercy.

The isolation of power did not disconcert Caesar. He required extraordinary powers to achieve his aims, and accepted the risks with equanimity. People were afraid of him, and there were two sides to the fear that he engendered; on the one hand there was the risk of assassination, but on the other there was the ready cooperation and obedience that most people evince when afraid of the consequences of the opposite course of action. Caesar no longer had time to waste on long-winded gentle persuasion. He underlined his power and influence by holding four triumphs at the end of September, though it was high summer in reality. The first was over Gaul, the second over Egypt, the third over Pharnaces and the fourth over Juba. There was no mention of Pompey, or of victories over any Romans, save that in the triumph over Juba, which stood for the African war, he made reference to the deaths of Cato and Scipio. In the first triumph, the axle of his chariot broke, and to conciliate the gods and turn the bad omen to good account, he mounted the steps of the Capitoline temple on his knees, which was in fact the method normally used by venerable Romans in the past.

There were splendid funeral games held belatedly in honour of his daughter Julia, and a public feast for the same cause, all of which had been promised when she died in 54. Apart from the feelings he entertained for his daughter and his wish to honour her memory, his credibility depended upon his being a man of his word, fulfilling his promises. There was another aspect of Julia's funeral games and feasting, in that she had been Pompey's wife. Few of the spectators would be able to disassociate the memory of Julia from the memory of Pompey. The Forum Julii was finally dedicated, though the building work had probably been finished some time before. The temple inside the Forum was promised to Venus Victrix before the battle of Pharsalus, but Caesar now dedicated it to Venus Genetrix, his illustrious if mythical ancestress.

For reasons which are best known to himself, he also erected a statue of Cleopatra opposite the goddess. It caused great resentment, giving rise to the suspicion that he intended to make Cleopatra his Queen, and that all Romans were to be made subject to her, or that she was going to be made a living goddess as Caesar was to be made a god. The presence of the Egyptian Queen in Rome and at Caesar's side was a political expedient. Cleopatra's primary concern was Egypt and its future, and she needed to create a viable relationship not only with Caesar but with Rome itself, to establish long-term recognition as friend and ally of the Roman people. Caesar was over fifty, and despite Egyptian Ptolemaic mythology derived from the Pharaohs, she herself was not immortal. The survival of Egypt as a free country beyond her own lifetime depended on establishing good relations with the foremost power in the Mediterranean world, and seeking approval for her son Caesarion, who blended Egypt and Rome in one ruler. Caesar acknowledged the boy as his own son, and after his death Antony presented Caesarion's claims to the Senate. The corollary to this was the fear that Cleopatra and Caesarion intended to rule Rome as well as Egypt. The rumours got out of hand, solidified into fact, and metamorphosed into justified hatred, so easily exploited by Octavian in the next decade.

Attending to business, the soldiers were among Caesar's first concerns. He initiated a settlement programme for the veterans, appointing legates to find land and make the arrangements for its purchase. He personally attended only to those cases which were not straightforward. He paid his agents well out of the funds derived from the vast amounts of booty brought home from the wars. The same source enabled him to pay donatives to the citizens as well. When the jealous soldiery complained about the amounts squandered on the populace, Caesar dealt harshly with them. According to Dio, he executed one man and had two more sacrificed to Mars, displaying their heads at the doors of the Regia, his official residence as Pontifex Maximus. This barbaric act has been attributed to the need to appeal to the religious beliefs of the mob, but a man who could authorise such an act was a man to be feared.

In a very short time, Caesar produced a staggering amount of legislation covering a wide range of subjects. The speed with which he performed all this work presupposes that he had already thought long and deeply about what was necessary to mould the Roman world into a workable whole. This was not one man working on a whim of the week basis, but one man at the head of a private committee, going through a series of measures already in draft form, probably dating from several years ago. Dealing with the people of Rome he enacted various measures designed to control the mob and to encourage the growth of population in the right quarters. He reduced the number of people entitled to receive the free corn dole instituted by Clodius, pruning the list of 320,000 names to 150,000, a figure that was not to be exceeded, which presumably entailed some sort of waiting list. He encouraged the growth of large families by means of rewards, to replace the men lost in the wars. Without unduly upsetting creditors, he passed laws to alleviate the problems of debtors. The cancellation of all debts was not feasible, but that had recently been the watchword of Dolabella and his circle, and the problem would not simply vanish, so Caesar had to make some response unless he wished to face riots such as Mark Antony had been forced to squash. Caesar also made some adjustments to the jury courts, restricting the panels to senators and equites, removing the *tribuni aerarii*, who had been allowed to share the responsibility of judgement since the consulship of Pompey and Crassus in 70. Provincial government was reformed and regulated. Praetors were to govern for one year and consuls for two years, something of an irony after all the fuss that Caesar had made over obtaining and extending his command in Gaul.

All this and more was pushed through at great speed and without the usual delaying tactics employed by his opponents. Caesar was in a position now where most of those who dared to oppose him were dead or absent, but he still took care to deny the opposition an opportunity to develop a voice. In drafting the legislation Caesar short-circuited senatorial debate altogether. He simply told senators what he had decided upon, giving no leeway for open discussion. Sometimes senatorial signatures were appended to documents when the men concerned had not even been present in the Senate, as Cicero complained in one of his letters. He said that the government of Rome was carried out in Caesar's house, which was absolutely correct. In Caesar's household, the bills for lamp-oil and ink must have been colossal.

The reform of the calendar for which Caesar is justly famous was long overdue. The lunar calendar used by the Romans had always required regular adjustments, with the intercalation of extra days; usually one month was inserted every two years. During the civil wars the instability of daily life had made it impossible to coordinate the intercalations, so that the seasons were out of sychronisation with the months. In order to rectify the current calendar, Caesar inserted 67 extra days into the year, adding the extra lunar month in February, and two more between November and December. Then from that year onwards, the lunar calendar was abandoned and the solar calendar was instituted, with 365 days to the year and one extra day to be inserted every four years. It is the basis of the calendar in use today, and it was not altered again until the eighteenth century. Cleopatra may have had some influence on the adoption of the solar calendar, since it was based on the

*29 Caesar as Dictator
for the fourth time.*
Drawn by Jaqui
Taylor

calculations of Egyptian astronomers, and implemented by Sosigenes, one of her influential courtiers.

The haste with which Caesar conducted all public business arose from the fact that the civil war had still not ended. The frenetic activity underscored his impatience to fight more battles in Spain, because the Pompeians who had survived were congregating there under Pompey's two sons Gnaeus and Sextus. Caesar planned to take Gaius Octavius with him, but the boy was ill, so the project had to be abandoned. Before he left, Caesar was made sole consul. He did not need any extra powers, but he had not had sufficient time to organise the consular elections, so this measure was to provide a stopgap to ensure that there was at least one consul, and to defer the elections, preserving the proper forms until he returned from Spain. There were scarcely any magistrates either, but Caesar's friend Marcus Aemilius Lepidus and eight specially appointed praetors were to attend to all business.

The Pompeians in Spain had recruited among the local population and raised a considerable army. Gnaeus Pompeius had arrived first, followed by his brother Sextus, and Labienus, who brought the fleet and the remaining troops from Africa. Caesar had sent his nephew Quintus Pedius, and Quintus Fabius Maximus to contain the Pompeians, but that was all they could hope to achieve without reinforcements, and without Caesar himself. Gnaeus was engaged in the siege of Ulia, south of Corduba where Sextus held the town with two legions, so the Caesarians had made camp east of Corduba, and remained there, unable to offer open battle. To add to the troops under Pedius and Fabius, Caesar now brought the Tenth legion, and the Fifth raised in Transalpine Gaul, and

30 *Gaius Octavius,*
   Caesar's great-nephew.
   The portrait may not be
   contemporary, and is an
   idealised portrayal,
   emphasising his youth.
   Courtesy Vatican
   Museums, Vatican
   City

nicknamed *Alaudae*, 'Larks'. In order to draw Gnaeus off from Ulia, Caesar laid siege to Corduba, threatening Sextus. The plan worked, but when he saw that he would be unable to reduce Corduba, and Gnaeus was not to be drawn into battle, Caesar determined to waste no more time on the project. As usual, the lack of supplies dictated the length of time he could remain in one place. He heard that the fortified town of Ategua, 20 miles south-east of Corduba, was protected by a Pompeian garrison but also housed vast stores of grain, so he set off to lay siege to it. The siege was marked by a horrific act by the garrison commander Munatius Plancus. He rounded up the Caesarian sympathisers among the citizens and massacred them, ordering the soldiers to throw the bodies over the town walls in full view of the besieging troops. Perhaps it was exhaustion and desperation that motivated the generals, but brutality was a feature of the second Spanish war whenever the two sides clashed.

The town of Ategua fell to Caesar after the garrison twice attempted and failed to break out through Caesar's lines. Gnaeus drew off, leaving the Pompeians to their fate. They surrendered. The two opposing armies chased each other from place to place with Gnaeus in the lead. The chase ended at Munda. The site has not been definitively identified, but was probably west of Urso, which Caesar later chose as a site for one of his many colonies. Here Gnaeus offered battle. Caesar had not expected this, so it was a repeat of the battle of Pharsalus, where he was in the middle of giving orders for breaking camp when he noticed the enemy formations, and seized the day. He gave the orders for attack. The details of this battle are not clear, except that it was hard fought. It seems that Gnaeus Pompeius had chosen his site well, and had every chance of winning the battle. There was a stream and a surrounding marshy area between the two armies, and the Caesarians had to cross it, thus delaying their progress. At one point Caesar had to dash to the front to rally his troops, then the Tenth legion featured as the main driving force of the attack, pushing the Pompeians back on their left wing. Gnaeus ordered Labienus to move from the right wing to assist the left, but before he got into position Caesar ordered up his ally king Bogud of Mauretania with his horsemen, who prevented Labienus from engaging and drove him off. The Pompeian line crumbled. The battle was won, but Caesar said afterwards that he had often struggled to achieve victory, but this was the first time that he had fought for his life. Gnaeus Pompeius escaped, but was captured and like his father he was decapitated. Sextus Pompeius fled from Corduba, leaving his two legions to their own devices. Caesar took the town amid tremendous slaughter.

The Pompeian cause refused to die in Spain, but while Caesar was there, marching from town to town, resistance subsided, largely because Caesar's measures to contain it were very harsh. On the other hand there were rewards for those communities which had been loyal to Caesar. Taxes were reduced and lands increased at the expense of the communities which had declared for the Pompeians. Some towns received Latin rights, and Caesar founded several colonies of Roman citizens with the obligation of defending their own territories and performing military service. During the last phase of the Munda campaign, while he settled communities and made his administrative arrangements, Caesar was accompanied by his great-nephew Gaius Octavius. Too late for the battle of Munda, Octavius arrived in Spain with a few companions and their slaves, among whom was his lifelong friend Marcus Vipsanius Agrippa. He acquitted himself well, and travelled back to Rome in Caesar's own litter. On the journey from Transalpine Gaul, the party was joined by Mark Antony, who was now back in favour, and destined for higher things in his career. He was to be consul with Caesar for 44.

8 The foot of Pompey's statue

The outcome of Caesar's activities in Spain was far different from Pompey's in the east, when he returned to seek ratification for his administrative arrangements. Caesar as Dictator did not feel the need to seek ratification. He had established colonies named after himself whose inhabitants would direct their allegiance to him rather that the Senate and People of Rome. As he had the authority to appoint governors and deploy legions, the armies too were Caesar's rather than Rome's, and the veterans in the colonies would also be his first and Rome's second. The wars too were his. When he had settled accounts with Pharnaces in the east he had installed a relative of his, Sextus Caesar, as governor of Syria, but the Pompeian Quintus Caecilius Bassus had emerged from hiding and taken over the province, intriguing to have Sextus Caesar murdered. The Caesarians Quintus Cornificius and then Gaius Antistius Vetus were sent to oust Bassus. Caesar could spare only two legions as reinforcements. It remained a purely Roman matter until Pacorus, the son of the king of Parthia, entered the scene and tipped the balance, expressing too strong an interest in the Roman provinces of the east. A war with Parthia loomed as soon as Caesar was free to turn his attention to it, and he intended to conduct it himself.

This great undertaking was put on hold while Caesar returned to Rome. He did not immediately enter the city, because he wanted to preserve the proper forms, not entering Rome as a general in command of an army until he held his triumph. He went instead to his estates at Labici, not far from the city, and there he wrote his will. The triumph was celebrated some short time later. It was officially over Spain, but this time, more than ever, it was transparently obvious that there had been no conquest except of the Pompeians. There was a protest from the tribune Pontius Aquila. When Caesar's triumphal chariot passed his seat, Aquila pointedly remained in it, not rising to greet the conquering hero. Caesar challenged Aquila: 'Make me give up the state, Aquila. After all you are tribune.' This response was from a man with little time to do what he thought he must do, impatient, and on a short fuse. A fit of pique was ill-suited to noble rule, but for days Caesar did not let the matter drop, adding to the end of every decree, discussion or decision the rider 'Provided that Pontius Aquila allows it'. He no doubt lost more credit than he gained by such behaviour. Similarly he lost more credit when he replied to Cicero's book extolling Cato as the noblest Roman of the Republic, the supreme statesman and consummate orator. The work was written at the behest of Marcus Brutus, who had been brought up as part of Cato's family, and who wrote a pamphlet of his own, generally acknowledged to be of lower literary merit than Cicero's work, but both are now lost. The portrait of his constant enemy as the paragon of Roman politics goaded Caesar into writing his *Anti-Cato*, pointing out all the less edifying qualities of the Republican hero, such as his over-fondness for wine, and the fact that when in need of money he had divorced his wife so that she could marry the orator Hortensius, and had taken money for the transaction. Caesar had never been able to win Cato over to his side, and now even after he was dead his old enemy could still win a following. Caesar's anger is understandable, but giving vent to his feelings in such a public way did nothing to convert his audience to his point of view. He would have done better to ignore Cicero's work, confining his opinions to dinner parties. It seemed that his famous *clementia* did not extend to Cato's shade.

The challenge to his authority did not stop Caesar from appointing magistrates and ordering the state to his satisfaction. He had received the command against the Parthians via a law of the people, and was concerned to fill all military posts and especially the public offices with his adherents, in order to direct policy while he was absent from Rome. He estimated that the campaign would take three years, since he intended first of all to make war on the troublesome Dacians across the Danube, then go to the east. Consequently he lined up his consular candidates for the years 44-41; he and Mark Antony were consuls for 44, Aulus Hirtius and Gaius Pansa were elected for 43, and Decimus Brutus and Lucius Munatius Plancus for 42. In December 45 when the new tribunes stepped into office, Mark Antony's brother Lucius Antonius passed a law granting Caesar the right to recommend half of all the candidates for office, except the consuls.

Most of the state was now in Caesar's hands. He controlled the armies and the finances, he appointed provincial governors, he recommended most of the candidates for office in Rome, and though the consuls were technically elected they were in reality his men. He could create new patricians and elevate men to the Senate, including recently enfranchised citizens from outlying parts of the Empire. He had founded colonies in Gaul, Spain, and Africa, and continued the policy of colonisation after the civil wars were over. By means of planting colonies he revived Corinth and Carthage, destroyed by the Romans half a century before he was born. Honours flowed in his direction, voted by the Senate, mounting almost by the hour. Fifty days' thanksgiving were voted after the victory at Munda, and anniversaries of his other victories were to be marked by festivals and games. He was granted the use of Imperator, commander, as a hereditary name. Appearances were important in Rome, and Caesar was to be distinguished by his triumphal clothes which he was entitled to wear on all public occasions, as well as a laurel wreath, which happily disguised his baldness. A temple was to be built to Libertas, Freedom, in his honour, and at the circus games an ivory statue of Caesar was to be carried along with those of the gods. A statue of him was to be set up in the temple of Quirinus, with an inscription 'to the unconquerable god'. These honours were greater than any hitherto accorded to one man, and Caesar readily accepted them. He was elevated far above his peers, and whilst no one could accuse Caesar of modesty or low self-esteem, it was perhaps only now that he began to take himself so seriously that he lost touch with reality.

His impatience with opposition may have derived from the fact that he had held onto a vision of what was good for Rome for so long that he now considered that all right-minded men must approve of what he would have termed blindingly obvious schemes. Many an ordinary individual has been totally perplexed by the fact that what is in their minds is not necessarily reflected in the minds of everyone else. But Caesar was not an ordinary individual. He had the power to make sure that other minds thought as he did, or perhaps not at all. His impatience also stemmed from his constant haste. He was in his mid-fifties, he was planning to go to Parthia, and there was still much to do in Rome. Settlement of his veterans was still going on and needed time and effort; building schemes in the city were in various stages of progress, among them the Senate House, replacing the old one burnt down at Clodius' funeral. Caesar also entertained great plans for the Campus Martius, where there was to be a new temple to Mars and a theatre, bigger and better than Pompey's.

Caesar may have had a long-term view of a reformed Rome and a reformed administration of the Empire, and certain liberal themes can be seen running through his legislation, but since he was cut down before he had finished the great work, and left no written plan, it is not possible to be certain that he was in fact endeavouring to produce a coherent whole out of the morass that Roman politics had sunk into. Current opinion favours the view that he could not find the ultimate solution to Rome's problems, and that he intended to conduct the Parthian war simply in order to escape the political turmoil. His friend Gaius Matius discussed the problems with Cicero after Caesar's death, expressing the view that if Caesar could not find the answer, then he doubted that anyone else could do so. Matius was a loyal friend, convinced of Caesar's genius, so it seems that even with all his advantages, that of autocracy and also intellectual brilliance, Caesar could not create out of Rome the Empire that he desired.

Autocracy was his aim, not least because it saved so much time. To his opponents that in itself was just about bearable, because there was still just a small chance that his autocracy might be temporary. Sulla had achieved what he set out to do and then retired. Even the knowledge that Caesar had said that Sulla must have been an idiot to lay down his powers need not be too depressing, since there was always hope that Caesar would rest contented when the state was running along the lines he laid down for it. He had been appointed Dictator for ten years in 46, a disturbing concept but not irreversible, since in 36 it might all come to an end, and then normal life could be resumed bit by bit. Caesar's third, fourth and fifth consulships from 46 to 44 could be viewed in the same light, as a necessary evil, held conjointly with the Dictatorship. His censorial powers embodied in his office as *praefectus morum* could be tolerated, almost, if they were to disappear along with the Dictatorship. But then came the Dictatorship for life, *Dictator perpetuo*. There was no possibility that he would ever lay down his powers after he accepted this honour, no possibility that Rome would ever be restored to the governance of the Senate and the leading men, no paths to promotion except through Caesar and his agents, no offices that were not for the most part filled by Caesar's adherents, or those who pretended to be his adherents in order to rise. There was no debate, no discussion, not even any real share in government, no place for individuality or initiative, and certainly nothing to be gained from holding opinions that differed from Caesar's.

There had already been murmurs of dissatisfaction while Caesar was in Spain. Mark Antony had been approached to sound him out about removing Caesar. While he was out of favour, he would seem the likely candidate for conversion to the cause, as a bitter casualty of Caesar's displeasure, but he was far from that. It is said that he never warned Caesar of what he had heard when he went to meet him on his return journey from Spain, but since nobody was with the two of them to vouch for what was discussed, it is equally possible that Antony went to meet Caesar with the express purpose of warning him, and then they both decided to pretend that he had said nothing. Absolutism runs the risk of assassination at all times, and Caesar knew it.

If he had any inkling of dissension he did not show it. He was probably protected from the knowledge that there was discontent by his entourage, who would filter information as a matter of course. Balbus and Oppius vetted one of Cicero's letters and advised him to modify it somewhat because it seemed to criticise the administration of Rome by Caesar's men while he was in Spain. It cannot have been an isolated example, but if there were more people who were treated in the same way, their intimate letters describing their experiences have not been preserved. Only Cicero stands as a contemporary voice to describe what it was like to deal with Caesar. On one occasion he was kept waiting by Caesar's entourage when he wanted to speak to him on behalf of a friend; when Caesar found out, he railed against the system that had grown up around him, concluding that if eminent men like Cicero were kept waiting, then he must be hated indeed.

Caesar in the last years of his life combined charisma and arrogance with his absolute power. To meet him personally was to be both overawed and charmed, as Cicero describes when Caesar visited the neighbouring villa of Marcius Philippus, who had married Atia, the widowed daughter of Caesar's sister Julia. Philippus had thus become the stepfather of the young Gaius Octavius. A visit by Caesar was probably a worse fate than a visit by Elizabeth I of England, who regularly ruined her courtiers by eating them out of house and home. There were about 2000 people accompanying Caesar, according to Cicero, who was horrified at the spectacle, especially when Caesar wandered over to his villa for lunch next day. Cicero wrote to Atticus that Caesar was not the sort of guest to whom one says voluntarily 'Do come back and see me sometime'. Even so the charisma and charm comes through, pervading Cicero's account. Cicero did not dislike Caesar the man, nor even Caesar the politician, but he thoroughly hated Caesar the autocrat.

Rumours that Caesar intended to be king had been circulating widely and wildly, and all sorts of omens were seen or engineered to that end. It may have been enemies who placed a diadem on one of his statues on the *rostra*, the speakers' platform near the Senate House, or it may have been his adherents who wished to precipitate the matter. The diadem was a symbol from the Greek world denoting monarchy. The tribunes Gaius Epidius Marullus and Lucius Caesetius Flavus removed it. The same pair arrested a man in the crowd who addressed Caesar as *Rex*, or king. Caesar replied that his name was Caesar, not Rex, referring to the ancient families who held that name. The situation was defused temporarily. But Caesar was angry with the tribunes, who had acted on their own authority and made judgements of their own about whether Caesar should be king, and it was probably this independence that Caesar objected to rather than the denial of kingship, which he would have preferred to deny himself. The tribunes responded to his anger with the statement that they were being prevented from exercising the rights of their office. Caesar declared his dissatisfaction with the two tribunes to the Senate and allowed the senators to depose them. He had come a long way in a short time since he had made a *casus belli* out of the violation of the sacrosanctity of tribunes.

It was known by early February 44 that Caesar had accepted the Dictatorship for life. A document of 9 February describes him as designated *Dictator perpetuo*, and by 14 February he had accepted it. Caesar's situation with regard to the kingship was made worse at a festival celebrated on 15 February, the Lupercalia, a fertility rite of extreme antiquity. The consul Antony took part in the ceremony, which entailed running round the streets of Rome with other young men, wearing only a loincloth, and striking people, especially young women, with goatskin thongs. The process was supposed to make the women fertile and bear sons for Rome. Antony would have enjoyed this part, but he had another role to play for Caesar. He carried a diadem with him, which he offered to Caesar when he approached his chair, offering him in effect the title and rank of king. Caesar refused it. The audience roared approval that he had rejected it. Antony offered it again, with the same result. Motives in this little scenario are obscure. It may have been an idea of Antony's, carried out without the prior knowledge of Caesar, to make him accept the kingship, or reject it in front of the whole of Rome. Alternatively Caesar may have put him up to it in order to test the waters of popular opinion, either seeking approval from the crowd if he accepted it and then assuming the diadem with relative immunity, or it may have been an attempt to kill off rumour altogether by a public demonstration that he definitely did not wish to be king.

Whatever he intended, the speculation did not cease, and all he had achieved was to compound the situation. He was occupied in preparations for the Dacian and the Parthian wars. As a preliminary he had sent his great-nephew Gaius Octavius to gain military experience among the legions already stationed in Macedonia. It was rumoured that he intended to make Octavius his master of horse, *magister equitum*, in place of Marcus Aemilius Lepidus. Antony had been given this post when he administered Rome and Italy in Caesar's absence. Octavius never took up the post, and there are doubts on the part of certain scholars that Caesar would have entrusted an adolescent, kinsman or not, with such a responsibility. It depends upon the extent to which Caesar intended to groom Octavius as his successor, a factor which cannot be known even with hindsight. The focus of attention would not be wholly upon Octavius at the time, since inflammatory stories began to circulate that Parthia could be conquered only by a king. Then followed the rumour that Lucius Cotta, a relative of Caesar's mother, was going to propose that Caesar should be made king of all the Roman world, except Rome itself.

The speculation was in effect purely one of semantics. The title of king had all the connotations of the hated rulers of the city after its foundation, antithetical to the idea of the Republic, but whatever he chose to call himself, Caesar was that already. He was in supreme power and he had no intention of giving it up. Dictator, king, sole consul, tyrant, none of this would disguise the fact that there was only one way to wrest Rome from Caesar's grasp. Men began to whisper about assassination; a conspiracy evolved. The foremost among the conspirators was Marcus Junius Brutus, the son of Caesar's mistress Servilia, now called Quintus Caepio Brutus after his adoption by his uncle Quintus Servilius Caepio. He had been brought up in the household of Cato and educated in philosophy and oratory; he held lofty ideals about the Republic. Given his background and his loyalty to Cato, he probably recoiled at the suggestion that since his mother and Caesar had been lovers, he could have been Caesar's natural son. Gaius Cassius Longinus was the next most ardent anti-Caesarian. He had fought on the side of Pompey and been pardoned by Caesar, but never really settled down in the shadow of Caesar's clemency. Then there were Caesarians like Decimus Brutus and Gaius Trebonius who had held commands under Caesar. Men who thought they should have advanced their careers a little faster probably also joined the conspiracy. There were perhaps sixty men who knew of the plot, but only a few of them are known by name.

The plotters, who called themselves Liberators, would have to act quickly. They could have chosen to wait until Caesar left for the east, or even until he came back, having tried to restore the Republic in some way before he returned. But more victories, especially over a foreign enemy, would only enhance Caesar's power. They could take the risk that he might die or be killed, but they could not take the risk that he might be successful. Once they had worked themselves up into a cold hatred and convinced themselves of the need to act, the conspirators could not wind down and wait upon events. Sooner or later a 'now or never' attitude would enter the proceedings, in order to get it over with. It was a heavy undertaking to kill someone, especially one so prominent, and more important, one to whom several of the conspirators owed their careers. There were Caesarians as well as pardoned but disgruntled Pompeians among the Liberators. Caesar was to leave for Parthia on 18 March. More significantly he had dismissed his bodyguard. There would never be a better opportunity. There was a meeting of the Senate planned for 15 March, in Pompey's theatre. The conspirators decided upon that date; they swore oaths of loyalty to themselves and Rome, and braced themselves for the event.

On the morning of 15 March, Caesar felt ill and decided not to attend the Senate, especially as his wife Calpurnia had some premonition of disaster. The conspirators perhaps had not thought of this possibility. If Caesar did not turn up, it would mean that they would all have to sit through a meeting with their daggers hidden somewhere about them,

31 Daggers at the Ides of March on a coin issued by Marcus Junius Brutus to commemorate the murder of Caesar. The cap of liberty is depicted between the daggers, and on the obverse (not shown) Brutus placed his own portrait. Drawn by Jacqui Taylor

and then go home and start again. And there were only three days left. Decimus Brutus was sent to persuade Caesar to attend the meeting. So Caesar arrived at Pompey's theatre with a man he thought his friend, and there he met his fellow consul Antony, who was drawn away for a conversation with Gaius Trebonius, another of Caesar's friends. Before he went into the meeting, Artemidorus of Cnidus presented Caesar with a scroll, trying to warn him of the danger, but Caesar never read scrolls when they were presented to him; they were given to a member of his staff to be read later. Spurinna the augur had warned Caesar of catastrophe of the Ides of March, but Caesar had scoffed; seeing him now he said to him, 'The Ides of March have come', meaning that nothing had come of the prophecy of doom. Spurinna, according to legend, replied 'But not yet gone, Caesar'. Inside Pompey's theatre, the conspirators were waiting. They had decided that all should strike a blow so that they should all share the responsibility for the murder. Caesar died from twenty-three stab wounds, pulling his cloak over his head as he fell at the foot of Pompey's statue.

There were many senators who were not aware of the plot to kill Caesar, so when they saw what was happening they fled, not knowing what was to happen next. The answer to that question was nothing. The Liberators had made no plans to fill the gap left by Caesar, no plans to take over the state with a cry that the tyrant was dead, no plans to remove all the adherents closest to Caesar who could themselves take over. And there were no plans to take over the troops to support them in their new-found supremacy, because after all that would have been to act like Caesar himself, in a high-handed and unorthodox manner. They had even decided to spare Antony, mainly at the behest of Brutus, though Cicero lamented the fact that the golden opportunity to kill him was lost.

32 *Octavian as son of divine Caesar. The date when Octavian began to advertise himself as* divi filius *is not unequivocally established, but it is probable that he did so immediately after accepting his inheritance. A series of coins bearing the legend* Divi Juli F *and depicting weapons and also agricultural implements has been dated to the period just after Philippi when the land settlements for the veterans were in operation.* Drawn by Jacqui Taylor

At first Antony and Caesar's other supporters could not know this, and presumably they went home to barricade their houses, expecting loud kicks at the door at any moment, closely followed by men with swords. When nothing happened, gradually they would find out the state of affairs, and begin to plan for the future themselves.

Antony was the only official in high office, being consul. He took charge as soon as he could, first securing armed assistance from Lepidus, who brought troops to the Tiber island. Then he convened the Senate on 17 March. The conspirators had gone to the Capitol and prepared for a siege, surprised that cries of joy that the tyrant was dead had not resounded through the streets of Rome. They had not worked out that the only people whose liberty had been seriously curtailed were themselves and men like them, who wished to rule the mob in Rome and the provincials in the time honoured exploitative manner. The vast majority in Rome mourned Caesar. It is to Antony's eternal credit that he kept his head and prevented a bloodbath in Rome and another civil war from breaking out there and then.

In the two days since Caesar's murder, Antony had been very busy. It is not known how he stood with Balbus and Oppius, but they would be

33 Divine Caesar on a coin issued by Octavian. Drawn by Jacqui Taylor

the first men whom he approached, or who may have approached him. Caesar's *clientelae* would be a useful source of support, so he cultivated them, as well as Caesar's secretaries and assistants, among whom was Faberius, the only one named in the sources. With these associates he was able to piece together some form of government. He did not call out the troops to line the streets, having learned the hard way when he suppressed the disturbances caused by Dolabella and his cronies over their chronic debts. But no doubt his soldiers were close by, and there was a prearranged signal should he find himself in difficulties. Antony let everyone have their say, so the meeting was a riotous one, but the outcome was as good as it was going to get in the circumstances. The restoration of law and order was of prime importance. Cicero proposed a general amnesty, and everyone breathed a sigh of relief when the motion was adopted. Common sense had won the day, but Cicero privately despaired; his verdict on the assassination was that the conspirators had planned with the courage of men but the understanding of boys. Perhaps he had not thought of asking them what they were going to do after Caesar was dead, assuming that it went without saying that they had formulated plans for the government of the Empire.

Antony came to a precarious understanding with the conspirators still barricaded on the Capitol. He sent his infant son to them as hostage, to indicate that there was no intention of storming the hill. Later he entertained the so-called Liberators to dinner. There was a major dilemma that he had to solve, and he steered a middle course with great skill. Caesar had been murdered, so the murderers ought to be punished. That would divide Rome into two factions once again and cause civil war. But if they were not punished, it was equivalent to declaring that they had been

*34 Portrait of Octavian on
   a coin.* Drawn by
   Jacqui Taylor

justified in killing the man they called tyrant, and if Caesar had been justly killed, then strictly speaking all his acts should be annulled. That would mean that most of the magistrates and provincial governors would have to be replaced. Nearly all the senators owed something to Caesar. So that course was not to be recommended, either. There was an armed neutrality, while Antony carried on the government of Rome along Caesarian lines. He used the notes that Caesar had left to put forward all the measures which had been planned but not implemented, perhaps selecting those he thought more useful than others. He also mixed up his financial accounts with Caesar's, and managed to pay off all his debts, so men began to feel suspicious that he had defrauded the state, but in view of the alternative of civil war, perhaps it did not matter too much.

Having established calm and order, Antony and the Senate ratified the terms of Caesar's will on 18 March. There was a sum of money for every Roman citizen in the city, and Caesar's gardens were to be opened to the public. There were legacies to most of the conspirators, and some for Antony, though he was not in the first rank of the legatees. Caesar had left a quarter of his fortune to his kinsmen Pedius and Pinarius, but the main beneficiary was Gaius Octavius, Caesar's great-nephew, currently at Apollonia in Macedonia with the legions destined for the Parthian campaign. In a codicil to his will, Caesar had adopted Octavius as his son. None of this was perhaps held to be of great significance. The youth was only nineteen years old; he had fought no battles and had no political experience; he was of a delicate disposition, and could withstand neither heat nor cold; he never went out in summer without a hat and in winter he wore lots of clothes to keep warm, and anyway he was always ill.

Antony and the Senate had more to think about than the teenage heir of Caesar.

There was the funeral to arrange, where emotions would run high. Antony made a speech, perhaps something akin to the words that Shakespeare chose for him, pointing out how honourable were the conspirators in their aims. Then there was the question of who should govern which provinces. It was essential to remove Brutus and Cassius from Rome, so they were given the task of administering the corn supply in Asia and Sicily. Antony chose Cisalpine Gaul, where he would be closer to Italy, exchanging his designated province of Macedonia, which had been part of Caesar's plans for the campaign first into Dacia and then into Parthia. For this exchange to work, Antony had to have a law passed to remove the governor that Caesar had chosen for Cisalpine Gaul, the conspirator Decimus Brutus, who had already gone to take up his post. Antony also commandeered the legions from Macedonia, since there would now be no need for them in a Parthian campaign.

In the midst of all these arrangements, the young Gaius Octavius returned to Rome. He had changed his name after his adoption to Gaius Julius Caesar, to which he should have added Octavianus, indicating that he had been adopted into the Julii Caesares from the Octavii. But he never used this name by which historians identify him. He had to make strenuous efforts to have the adoption ratified by law, because testamentary adoption may not have been strictly legal, and he had to establish a firm basis for his use of Caesar's name. He devoted considerable efforts to gathering political support; he took over as many of Caesar's *clientelae* as he could and secured the services of Cornelius Balbus, a valuable ally who was Caesar's right-hand man. Ultimately he acquired an army with which to shore up his position. Reticent and cautious, Octavian was never shy and retiring, and he utilised to good effect Caesar's divinity. If not actually a living god, Caesar had been destined for deification after his death, a fact that Octavian did not allow the Roman populace to forget. He called himself *divi Juli filius*, or simply *divi filius*, eventually issuing coins bearing this proud legend.

Octavian had accepted his position as Caesar's heir, and clung to it tenaciously through the next fifty years, reshaping the Empire slowly and patiently, perhaps along the lines that Caesar had in mind, though with much less haste. Caesar was a man in a hurry, and in his frenetic desire for rapid results he abandoned tradition and rode roughshod over those who clung to it. Octavian was more fortunate in that he could allow so much more time for achieving what he wanted, and in 27 BC a grateful Senate renamed him Augustus. Thus it was that the conspirators rid themselves of the man who would be king, and gave the Roman world an Emperor.

35 *Statue of Augustus from Prima Porta. It dates from after 20, when Augustus had successfully negotiated with the Parthians for the return of the standards captured in 53 when Crassus was defeated. This is the legacy of Julius Caesar, Octavian-Augustus as the first of the Emperors of Rome. The elaborate armour emphasises military success, and the barefoot stance equates the ruler with the gods. The formula was to last for many centuries thereafter.* Courtesy Vatican Museums, Vatican City

Bibliography

Contemporary literature on Caesar is not abundant, but the extant texts are detailed and intense. Caesar's Commentaries on the Gallic War, and the Civil Wars, were begun by the general himself but completed by one of his officers, most probably Aulus Hirtius, who no doubt had access to Caesar's own notes and perhaps had conversed with him about several campaigns. The Commentaries serve as a vehicle for spreading Caesar's fame, and in consequence they are naturally full of self-advertisement, but not necessarily full of untruths. Elaboration on the one hand and omissions on the other may serve to distort the accounts of the wars, but on the whole the works are probably to be taken at face value, noting the names of officers and individual soldiers whose exploits were exceptional, and above all explaining mishaps and errors of judgement on the part of Caesar himself. Since none of the near disasters led to total failure, Caesar could afford to relate the preliminary misfortunes, and by means of the contrast between dire straits and eventual success he could enhance his own reputation as a commander of genius and luck.

Cicero's letters to his friends provide a detailed personal view of Caesar, or at least those episodes of his political life that Cicero chose to describe in his letters. There are several gaps, of course, especially during the early years when Caesar was absent in Spain and later when Cicero was in exile. There is a dearth of news on those occasions when Cicero and Atticus were both in Rome, and consequently did not need to write to each other. Much of the information relays current beliefs and assumptions and Cicero's own opinions; rarely is Caesar present in the flesh, but on the occasions when he is so described, the literary portrait is vivid and immediate, the Roman equivalent of archive footage for film and TV; for those who wish to find out what it was like to meet Caesar, Cicero's letters are as good as it gets.

Augustus and the Emperors who followed him were unlikely to allow the name of Caesar to be forgotten, but Augustus in particular needed to divorce himself from the image of Caesar the Dictator and from the series of civil wars that had brought him to power. Thus there is a gap of over a century between Cicero's work and the later Latin and Greek biographies and histories. These include Plutarch's life of Caesar in his comparisons of Greek and Roman politicians and generals, written probably during the reign of Trajan. Suetonius' biography, in his *Twelve Caesars*, was composed in the reign of Hadrian. His near contemporary Appian included an account of the civil wars in his *Roman History*, written in Greek in the reign of Antontius Pius, and in Severus' reign Cassius Dio recounted the story in his historical work, in the annalistic tradition, year by year. The surviving sections of the early part of his work cover the period from 69 BC to the mid-first century AD; the sources that he used have not been fully established.

Secondary sources abound, and a complete list would fill several pages. Apart from biographical works there are significant historical accounts of the period that serve to explain and illustrate the tumultuous times in which Caesar lived. Some of them are included in this selective bibliography.

Primary sources available in translation

Caesar *The Alexandrian, African and Spanish Wars*. Loeb Classical Library
Caesar *The Civil Wars*. Loeb Classical Library
Caesar *The Gallic Wars*. Loeb Classical Library
Cicero *Letters to Atticus* 3 vols. Loeb Classical Library
Cicero *Letters to his Friends* 3 vols. Loeb Classical Library
Dio *Roman History* 9 vols. Loeb Classical Library
Plutarch Life of Caesar in *Parallel Lives*. Loeb Classical Library
Suetonius *Twelve Caesars*. Loeb Classical Library
Sabben-Clare, J. (ed.) *Caesar and Roman Politics 60-50 BC: source material in translation*. Oxford University Press. 1971

Secondary sources

Beard, M. and Crawford, M. *Rome in the Late Republic: problems and interpretations*. London: Duckworth. 1985
Brunt, P.A. *Social Conflicts in the Roman Republic*. New York: W.W. Norton and Co. 1971
Cambridge Ancient History, Volume IX *The Roman Republic*. Cambridge University Press. 1932; reprinted with corrections 1951
Fuller, Maj. Gen. J.F.C. *Julius Caesar: man, soldier and tyrant*. London: Eyre and Spottiswoode. 1965
Gelzer, M. *Caesar: politician and statesman*. Harvard University Press. 1968
Grant, M. *Caesar*. London: Weidenfeld and Nicolson. 1974

Gruen, E.S. *The Last Generation of the Roman Republic.* University of California Press. 1974

Meier, C. *Caesar.* London: Harper Collins. 1995

Shotter, D. *The Fall of the Roman Republic.* London: Routledge.1994

Smith, R.E. *The Failure of the Roman Republic.* New York; Russell and Russell. 1955

Syme, R. *The Roman Revolution.* Oxford University Press. 1939

Taylor, L.R. *Party Politics in the Age of Caesar.* University of California Press. 1949

Index

Entries in **bold** denote illustrations